C000212935

A practical guide to
country
walking

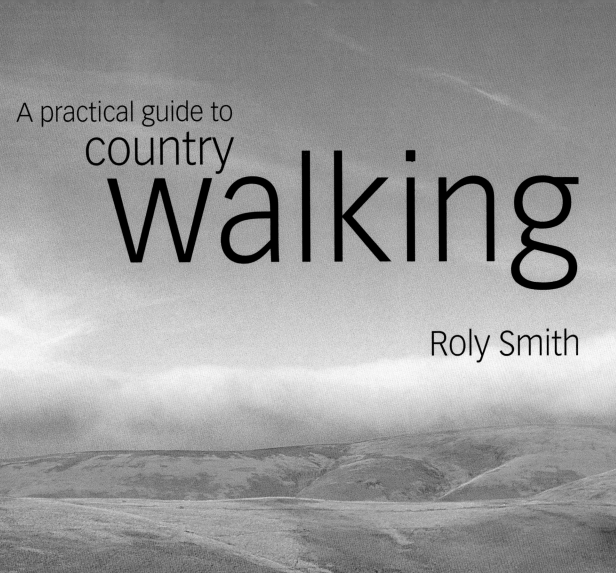

A practical guide to
country
walking

Roly Smith

HAMLYN

Publishing Director: Laura Bamford
Senior Editor: Trevor Davies
Art Director: Keith Martin
Senior Designer: Geoff Fennell
Design: Martin Topping
Production Controller: Joanna Walker
Picture Research: Sally Claxton and Christine Junemann

Acknowledgements

The author would like to thank Clive Allen – Marketing Man-
ager, Lowe Alpine; Jerry Gore – Marketing Director, Cotswold
Camping; Philip Round – Press Officer, Ordnance Survey;
Tony Wale – Silva (UK) Ltd, and David Bellamy.

The editor would like to thank the Ramblers Association;
Walt Unsworth at Cicerone; Christine Junemann for her help
in picture researching this project, and of course Roly Smith
whose enthusiasm and hard work on this book cost him
many precious months away from the footpaths of Britain.

First published in Great Britain in 1999
by Hamlyn, an imprint of
Octopus Publishing Group Limited
Michelin House, 81 Fulham Road, London SW3 6RB

Copyright © 1999 Octopus Publishing Group Limited

ISBN 0 600 59692 3

All rights reserved. No part of this publication may be reproduced,
stored in a retrieval system, or transmitted in any form or by any
means, mechanical, photocopying, recording or otherwise, without
the permission of the copyright holders.

A catalogue record for this book is available from the British Library

Produced by Toppan
Printed in China

CONTENTS

INTRODUCTION

More people are walking for pleasure than ever before, and it's not hard to see why. Walking is the easiest, cheapest and most practical form of exercise in the world. You can do it wherever you live and you don't have to spend a fortune on equipment. And there's another important plus – you don't need any specialist training.

THE BENEFITS
OF WALKING

All the experts agree that exercise is good for you. It lowers blood pressure and cholesterol levels, and improves the function of the heart and lungs. But what sort of exercise should you take?

In the 1970s and 1980s, jogging became very popular, but there was a high drop-out rate among beginners who suffered various injuries. Common complaints included ankle and knee strains and stress fractures, all due to the constant pounding of feet on hard pavements. To top it all, there was the sad story of the greatest proponent of jogging, Jim Fixx, who actually dropped down dead while out on a run.

The alternatives

Swimming is fine, if you can spare the necessary time and have easy access to a swimming pool. Cycling, although undoubtedly enjoyable and health-giving, can be potentially dangerous, especially in the heavy traffic which is the curse of our modern roads.

The best medicine

Thomas Jefferson, third president of the USA, declared that 'of all exercises walking is the best', and it was the Greek physician and 'Father of Medi-

A family group enjoying a healthy stroll through the autumn countryside. Walking is the healthiest form of exercise.

cine', Hippocrates, who first encapsulated the benefits of walking in the maxim: 'Walking is the best medicine'.

The great English historian George Macaulay Trevelyan wrote, in a famous essay on walking published in 1913, that he only had need of two doctors – his left leg and his right. *'When body and mind are out of gear (and those twin parts of me live at such*

close quarters that the one always catches melancholy from the other) I know that I shall have only to call in my doctors and I shall be well again.'

This view was echoed by American naturalist Henry David Thoreau, who wrote: *'I think that I cannot preserve my health and spirits unless I spend four hours a day at least – and it is commonly more than that – sauntering through the woods and over the hills and fields, absolutely free from all worldly engagements.'*

Mental benefits

It is now also accepted that walking has therapeutic properties which are beneficial on the mind. For many people, including some of the world's great thinkers, walking clears the mind and relieves the pressures of that modern killer: stress. A walk in the country can alleviate anxiety better than any tranquillizer.

The English writer Leslie Stephen, noting that many great men of letters had been keen walkers, claimed that

'Walking is the natural recreation for a man who desires not absolutely to suppress his intellect but to turn it out to play for a season.'

Wordsworth

William Wordsworth, the great poet of the English Lake District, composed many of his works while out walking. His opium-influenced friend, Thomas De Quincey, estimated that Wordsworth had covered between 280,000 and 290,000 kilometres (175,000–180,000 miles) on foot in his lifetime, and that walking was *'a mode of exertion which, to him, stood in the stead of alcohol and all other stimulants whatsoever to the animal spirits; to which, indeed, he was indebted for a life of unclouded happiness, and we for much of what is most excellent in his writings.'*

Was there perhaps a note of envy in the words of De Quincey?

Walking can give mental as well as physical benefits. This reflective walker is enjoying a fine view at the end of a perfect day.

THE HISTORY OF WALKING

No one can be sure who was the first person who took a walk just for pleasure. Maybe it was a Stone Age man who, perhaps after a successful mammoth hunt and feast, left his cave for a stroll to admire the wilderness of his virgin world.

The first ramblers

If we omit the enforced pedestrians who included the pilgrims and travellers of ancient times, perhaps the earliest walkers for pleasure were the 18th and 19th century tourers on foot, such

JOIN THE YOUTH HOSTELS ASSOCIATION
AND KNOW YOUR COUNTRY
THE MORE MEMBERS · THE MORE HOSTELS

APPLY TO:
THE HON SECRETARY
18 BRIDGE ROAD
WELWYN GARDEN CITY
NATIONAL OFFICE

MEMBERSHIP SUBSCRIPTION:
2/6 FOR THOSE UNDER 25 YEARS OF AGE
5/- FOR THOSE OVER 25
OVERNIGHT HOSTEL CHARGE 1/-

APPLY TO:
REGIONAL AREA OFFICE

as the Lutheran pastor from Berlin, Karl Moritz, who undertook a walking tour of England in 1782. His mode of travel was regarded as so unusual that he was often refused admission to local inns as appearing to be "some poor travelling creature."

The poets and writers of the Romantic Movement of the 18th and 19th centuries, including the French writer and philosopher Jean-Jacques Rousseau and followers of the Wordsworth school in the English Lake District, walked to commune with nature and receive inspiration for their works. Later nature writers such as the Americans Henry David Thoreau, Walt Whitman and John Muir all acknowledged their debt to walking as the best way to keep in touch with the natural world.

Several Victorian writers, including John Ruskin and Charles Dickens, were also great – and fast – walkers, and Ruskin advised: '*Of simple exercises, learn to walk and run at the utmost speed consistent with health: do this always going at the quickest pace you can.*'

Getting organised

Organised rambling (as leisure walking is known in Britain) started around the turn of the 19th century in the new industrial towns and cities of Britain. The Enclosure Acts of the early 19th century had resulted in much of what was previously common land being appropriated by the new landlords, and footpath preservation societies were formed to fight for ramblers' rights. All this came to a head with the infamous Mass Trespass on the forbidden moorland of Kinder Scout in April, 1932, after which five ramblers were imprisoned. In 1931, the British National Council of Ramblers' Federations was set up, and in 1935, this became the Ramblers' Association, which now has over 125,000 members, many of whom belong to organised walking clubs. The RA fights to keep open and accessible the network 225,000 kilometres (140,000 miles) of rights of

An early promotional poster, for the Youth Hostels Association, showing a healthy young couple striding out to the next hostel.

way in England and Wales, which are the main highways for Britain's growing army of walkers, and a similar job is done by the European Federation of Ramblers based in Kassel, Germany.

The formation of National Parks, starting with Yellowstone in Wyoming in the USA in 1872 and followed nearly 80 years later by the Peak District in Britain, promoted interest in country walking. The creation of long

Young ramblers from the Thirties seem to be getting directions from the village blacksmith.

distance paths, such as the Appalachian Trail up the eastern seaboard of the USA, have also greatly encouraged walking as a leisure pursuit. In fact, the Pennine Way and all the other National Trails in the world were based on the Appalachian Trail, and these way-marked trails are gaining in popularity.

Ten famous literary walkers

1. Jean-Jacques Rousseau (1712–78), French writer and philosopher
2. Thomas Jefferson (1743–1826), American President
3. William Wordsworth (1770–1850), English Poet Laureate
4. Samuel Taylor Coleridge (1772–1834), English poet and philosopher
5. Thomas De Quincey (1785–1859), English critic and essayist
6. Charles Dickens (1812–70), English novelist
7. Henry David Thoreau (1817–62), American naturalist and writer
8. Walt Whitman (1818–92), American poet
9. John Ruskin (1819–1900), English author and critic
10. George Macaulay Trevelyan (1876–1962), English historian

TYPES OF WALKS

So you've decided that walking is for you. But where to walk? There are many options, ranging from walking around the block during your lunch-hour in town to strenuous back-packing trips which require experience, stamina and a fair amount of preparation. Let's start by looking at the various levels of walking and what they can offer the would-be walker.

LOWLAND WALKING

Easily the most popular form of walking is the gentle stroll through the neighbouring country-side. This usually means keeping to rights-of-way which are established – legal footpaths, often way-marked and signed.

Open areas, such as country parks or areas where there is unrestricted access, are often found on the edge of towns or cities. Increasingly, in both Britain and America, former railway tracks have been converted to easy walking routes.

Walk away from stress

Many people find that these undemanding strolls are a valuable and convenient release from the everyday strains of their urban lives. They give you the opportunity to forget about the cares and concerns of work, and to 'get back to nature'. They can refresh both the mind and the body, and give you the chance to sort out your problems as you relax in the countryside.

Walking by water

Included in lowland walking are pleasant strolls by the river or canal bank, by the shores of a lake or reservoir, or following the coastline by the sea. The presence of water can have a tremendously refreshing and calming effect on the walker – it is a 'landscape' which is always changing, reflecting the moods of the sky and the weather. Sometimes the surface conditions of walking by the water can be taxing – if the bank or shore is muddy, for example, or you are passing through long stretches of shingle or sandy beaches.

Walking by the water has several other bonuses. Bird life is nearly always more interesting by the water, so don't forget your binoculars.

Walking in the lowlands imposes certain responsibilities on the walker. For example, gates should be shut after you.

One of the most pleasant forms of walking in the lowlands is in your local country park. Here a family group enjoy a stroll along a bracken-lined path.

Lakes and rivers provide their own specialist habitat for many water-dependent species of ducks and geese, while watching seabirds from a coastal cliff near to nest sites is one of the great thrills of bird-watching.

The ever-changing light also creates boundless opportunities for the photographer or artist – and there's always the chance of a paddle or swim if it gets too hot (see also *Coastal walking*, page 98).

Walking in the woods

Another form of lowland walking which can be very rewarding is woodland walking. This is particularly enjoyable on a hot summer's day when the shade of the

trees gives welcome relief, and the dappled light creates an enchanting picture on the forest floor.

Woodland walking is usually done on well-defined tracks or rides, so there's little chance of getting lost, and you can relax and enjoy the sights, sounds and smells of this leafy habitat. Trees also attract their own types of wildlife, and the patient – and, more importantly, quiet – walker may be rewarded with unforgettable glimpses of deer and other large woodland animals, as well as abundant bird life (see also *Forest Walking*, page 96).

In cultivated lowland countryside, many paths and tracks are well-marked, and good distances can be chalked up as you stride across the grain of the land.

The relaxing allure of inland waterways. However, many of the paths alongside rivers and streams can be heavy going.

UPLAND WALKING

'Great things are done when men and mountains meet: These are not done by jostling in the street.'

So wrote the great English poet and artist William Blake, and the attraction of walking in the hills has a long tradition.

At this point, the distinction must be drawn between climbing and walking; although much mountain walking does include climbing uphill, in this book we will be concerned only with walking. Climbing is a quite separate, though connected, pastime which in simple terms involves equipment such as helmet and ropes, and the use of hands as well as feet to ascend rock faces.

Rise to the challenge

Mountain or hill walking is one of the most rewarding branches of the hobby, but it is also the most demanding and potentially dangerous for the ill-prepared or unequipped. To take all day to ascend to a shapely summit and admire a stupendous view across the surrounding countryside is one of the greatest joys for the walker. But such rewards are not easily won, and such day-long uphill walks are much more arduous than the lowland strolls described earlier (see also section on uphill walking , page 94)

A certain level of basic fitness is required, in addition to specialist, waterproof clothing and sturdy footwear. Knowledge and experience of using a map and compass are also essential before you set out on a hill or mountain walk. For these reasons hill walks are not recommended for beginners, but they are something that a novice can quickly attain having first mastered the intricacies of lowland walking.

Safety first

Safety is a key factor in hill walking because not only is

The freedom of the hills. A walker strides out at the top of this steep climb from a valley in the English Lake District.

the terrain potentially more dangerous, with steep slopes and long drops where a mistake can sometimes be fatal, but also the weather conditions can change dramatically in the course of a day's walk in the hills.

This is where the right equipment, and most imortantly the right clothing, footwear and navigation instruments, becomes vitally important. Details of these will be discussed in Chapter

4, but suffice to say that getting lost or experiencing a good soaking while walking in the hills can be life threatening. Most calls to mountain rescue teams are not to help hardy mountain climbers who have fallen from cliff faces, but to inexperienced or badly-equipped hill walkers who have severely overestimated their own abilities.

Another fine view of the Lake District. A mother and her children enjoy the moment as they look over mountain and lake.

There are several levels and types of upland walking. These range from following a well-marked trail on a popular peak to more serious ridge walking and 'horseshoe' walks around a range of hills in a day. Longer mountain treks will be described on the following pages. Everywhere you walk in the hills, the going is rougher, stonier and tougher than it is in the surrounding lowlands. The rigours of such landscapes make good equipment essential.

Enjoying a high-level path along the edge of a mountain valley is one of the great joys of hill walking.

The hill walker can really 'get away from it all' on a trek into the mountains, where the presence of nature and the feeling of wilderness are experienced much more strongly than when in the lowlands. While the risks of walking in the hills are obviously greater than in the lowlands, the rewards are immeasurably greater too.

Backpackers high in the hills on a mountain expedition must ensure that they have everything with them.

BACKPACKING AND LONG-DISTANCE WALKING

Once you have mastered the essentials of walking in the lowlands and the hills, it is often a natural progression to move on to longer walks taking several days, which will obviously require overnight stops.

These long-distance paths, or National Trails as the official LDPs are known in the USA and now in Britain also, are a much more severe test of the walker's stamina. They often take you into wilder country, far from civilisation. You must therefore be experienced and well-prepared before you embark upon your first long-distance walk.

walks, especially in the uplands. Backpacking also requires a higher level of fitness than ordinary day-walking, because you have to carry all your camping equipment on your back with you – and this can be a considerable burden for the inexperienced walker.

Details of the equipment required for backpacking trips will be described in Chapters 5 and 7.

Backpacking

While some walkers will wish to use local facilities for overnight accommodation, others prefer to carry their accommodation with them, camping out overnight wherever they end up after a day's walking. This is known as backpacking and requires specialist equipment, such as a tent and cooking equipment, and the knowledge of how to use it.

For many walkers, backpacking is the ultimate countryside or wilderness experience – feeling that you are actually becoming a part of the landscape through which you are walking, and enjoying nature at first hand. But it is not for the inexperienced or first-time walker, and an apprenticeship should first be served on longer single-day

Some trails to try

All National Trails are based on the original idea of the 3,379-kilometre (2,100-mile) Appalachian Trial which runs up the eastern coast of the USA from Maine to Georgia. This was the brainchild of forester Benton MacKaye, who founded the Appalachian Trail Conference and saw its eventual completion in 1937.

The Appalachian Trail is one of the longest way-marked footpaths in the world, and winds through eight National Forests and six National Parks, skirting mountain streams and lakes and going through hundreds of miles of natural broad-leaved forest. Other popular American trails include the 4,119-kilometre (2,560-mile) Pacific Crest Trail, a serious mountain

A couple of backpackers head for the hills hand-in-hand on a mountain excursion in Norway.

walk from Mexico to Canada, the 4,988-kilometre (3,100-mile) Continental Divide Scenic Trail, which follows this significant geological feature through the states of Montana, Wyoming, Colorado, and New Mexico, and the 2,091-kilometre (1,300-mile) Florida Scenic Trail.

In Europe, the Tour du Mont Blanc is a 116-kilometre (72-mile) long high-level route well served with mountain huts and encircles the highest point in the Alps, and the E1 route crosses the Continent on its 2,767 kilometres (1,740 miles) to link the North Sea with the Mediterranean. Two popular Irish routes are the 183-kilometre (114-mile) Dingle Way around the Dingle Peninsula in the south west of Ireland, and the 917-kilometre (570-mile) Ulster Way which is a circular route around the six counties of Northern Ireland, including the fabulous Antrim Coast.

British examples include the 434-kilometre (270-mile) Pennine Way, which runs up the highest point of the Pennines and Cheviots from Edale in the Peak District to Kirk Yetholm just across the Scottish Border; and the 829-kilometre (515-mile) South West Coast Path, which runs around the south west peninsula from Minehead in Somerset to Poole in Dorset.

The advantage of the official long-distance trails is that they are often well signed and way-marked and there is plentiful accommodation – from camp sites and youth hostels to bed and breakfast and hotel accommodation - en route. They will also take you through some of the finest countryside – just made for walking.

Ten classic backpacking trails

1. The Appalachian Trail – 3,379 kilometres from Maine to Georgia, eastern USA

2. The Pacific Crest Trail – 4,119 kilometres from Mexico to the Canadian Border

3. The Milford Track – 53 kilometres from Lake Te Anau to Milford Sound, New Zealand

4. The E1 – 2,767 kilometres from the North Sea to the Mediterranean, across Europe

5. The Tour du Mont Blanc – 116 kilometres around Europe's highest peak

6. The Pennine Way – 434 kilometres from Edale to Kirk Yetholm, Great Britain

7. The South West Coast Path – 829 kilometres from Minehead to Poole, England

8. The West Highland Way – 150 kilometres from Glasgow to Fort William, Scotland

9. The Dingle Way – 183 kilometres around the Dingle Peninsula, Ireland

10. The Ulster Way – 917 kilometres around the six counties of Northern Ireland

One of the benefits of urban walking is that the ground is usually suitable for prams enabling the whole family to enjoy the walk.

URBAN WALKING

Most of us live in towns and cities these days, and for many of us 'townies' the opportunities for getting out for a walk are pretty limited. We travel to work by car, bus or train, only have an hour for lunch. This seems to leave only the weekend for walking.

But our urban lifestyles needn't mean that we can't stretch our legs a bit further than the walk to the car park, bus stop or train station before and after work. There is much to be said for a brisk walk around the block during the lunch hour, or perhaps walking to the next bus stop, rather than the first one, on the way home.

City stroll

Urban walking, it has to be said, is an acquired taste, although authors such as Charles Dickens have sworn by its benefits. In *The Uncommercial Traveller*, Dickens recounts how a bout of insomnia caused him to walk the streets of Victorian London for several nights. His disorder was soon cured by his nightime strolls, and he returned home refreshed but tired by sunrise. He called this experiment 'houselessness' and concluded:

'I knew well enough where to find vice and misfortune of all kinds, if I had chosen; but they were put out of sight, and my houselessness had many miles upon miles of streets in which it could, and did, have its own solitary way.'

A new perspective

Walking the streets of a large town or city gives the walker a completely different perspective from that of the car or bus passenger. The first thing you notice is the architecture which makes up the streets. Looking up above the bright, neon-lit fascias of the shop fronts can often provide an insight into the architectural fashions of bygone eras. And exploring the alleyways and side streets can show sides of a city that the tourist never sees. You also meet more people, and feel more intimately the pulse of the city at whatever time of the night or day you take your walk.

One of the best ways of exploring the 'hidden' face of a city is to follow the local waterways. Birmingham, in the English Midlands, is a good example of this, and the city council has in recent years recognised the importance of its canal towpaths as a recreational resource, and has done much to improve them. Did you know, for example, that Birmingham has more miles of canals than Venice?

Urban churchyards, parks and gardens are also places to explore and enjoy on foot. A brisk walk around your local park can be just as invigorating as a country walk, especially because of the contrast it provides with its surrounding urban environment. These places are often referred to as the lungs of the city, but it is your own lungs that will benefit from exploring such areas as you take time out from the hustle and bustle of city living. And the other advantage of urban walking is that you need no equipment at all. All you need is the will to put your best foot forward.

Take a friend

Cities can be dangerous places and many people, particularly women, will feel vulnerable walking alone in town. Whenever possible you should try to walk with a companion. Not only will you feel safer, but also you will have somebody to share your urban stroll with.

You should avoid walking alone in any environment. Even minor setbacks like a sprained ankle can turn a solo walk into a disaster.

Having a dog as a pet is a good excuse for taking regular, urban walks. This way, both you and your pet keep fit.

FITNESS AND SPORT WALKING

A growing number of enthusiasts, especially in the USA, are taking up walking primarily as an aid to fitness – in much the same way that jogging became popular in the 1970s.

This type of walking is known as fitness or sport walking, and it requires more discipline than any of the types of walking we have looked at so far.

Quick step

Whereas in walking for pleasure you set your own pace, fitness walking demands the setting up of a specific programme for regular, and essentially fast, walking to suit your individual lifestyle. For maximum benefit, the walker should walk fast enough to get the heart rate up to 70-80 per cent of its capacity – termed the target heart rate – so producing the desired aerobic effect on the body. Your individual target heart rate will depend on your own age and fitness levels, and it is worked out by taking your pulse and calculating the figure from a set formula.

Regularity is also very important in fitness walking. To obtain the full benefits, you need to walk at least three times a week – maintaining that fast, aerobically-effective pace, swinging your arms naturally – for at least 20-30 minutes during each session.

What is an aerobic pace? The official description is 'brisk' – or the kind of walking you might do if you were

The fun of walking for fitness can be improved significantly if you do it with a friend or with your partner.

A fitness walker strides out beside a lake. Good footwear is vitally important when you are walking on hard pavements.

late for an appointment. Most people achieve this at about 120 steps per minute, the equivalent of five to six kilometres per hour (3-4 miles per hour).

The next step up from fitness walking is pace walking, in which, as the name suggests, a faster pace is maintained, swinging your arms backwards and forwards across your chest in an exaggerated fashion, and using them in rhythmic concert with the legs.

Walking as a sport

At its extreme, walking enters the realm of true sport or athletics. Power walking, for example, applies the principle of progressive resistance to walking. It involves the carrying of weights on your wrists and ankles and/or a weighted rucksack, and deliberately takes in steep hills on route. Maximum aerobic benefits are obtained by using a faster pace, longer stride and deep, rhythmic breathing.

Inevitably, these personal challenges can lead into the competitive fields of sport and race walking, which are really outside the scope of this book. Basically, race walking rules demand that one foot always maintains contact with the ground, and that the leg supporting the body is straightened on each stride. Special athletics coaching is usually required for competitive sport or race walking, which can see participants reach speeds of between eight and ten kilometres an hour (5-8 miles per hour).

With all these extensions from walking for pleasure, it is important to build up your pace slowly, carry water to prevent dehydration if the weather is hot, and slow down gradually at the end of the exercise. And as most of these activities are performed on hard pavements in town or on race tracks, it is important to wear supportive and cushioned footwear, such as good quality athletics shoes or spikes.

FAMILY WALKING AND STROLLING

A stroll in the country can be one of the most enjoyable ways to spend time with one's family. And it's hardly surprising, given the fact that it is with our family that most of first learned to walk. Those first staggering steps clinging to the hand of a convenient parent soon develop into a confident stride and full-scale family outings into the countryside.

Family walking, is a key aspect of the hobby, particularly when combined with a visit to attractive countryside with perhaps a picnic en route.

The essence of family walking: Grandad finds a family stroll a healthy way to spend time with his grand daughters.

Give me a hand, Dad! A family group pick their way across marshy ground while out on a ramble.

Setting the pace

As always with walking in groups, the pace of the walking must be geared to the slowest member, usually the youngest child in a family situation. That shouldn't mean that the parents or the older children will get bored, because they can share in the constant thrill of discovery which is one of the great joys of walking with children.

Realistic targets

A strict limit should always be fixed on the length of such walks, again depending on the ability of the least experienced or youngest members of the family. Too long or too ambitious a walk can result in accusations of a 'route march' and will demoralise the 'troops'.

So pick a route which is easy and comfortably attainable by all members of the family, with not too many hills or steep ascents, and a number of possible stopping and resting places. There should be points of interest, such as a building of historical importance, or an interesting landscape feature, or wildlife. With younger walkers, the cry of 'Are we there yet?' or 'How much further is it?' can come quite early into a walk.

Of course, really young children will have to be carried all the way by Dad or Mum, in a papoose or other kind of specialist rucksack (see page 60). It is amazing how babies soon adapt to this kind of travel, often dropping off to sleep quite quickly, despite (or because of) the constant rocking and rolling motion.

A little bribery

Incentives – and sometimes downright bribery – are very important when walking with children. When an objective, such as a car park, hilltop or other feature, comes into view, it's not a bad idea to suggest that such a place would be a convenient spot for a rest, food or drink. This also gives the children a greater sense of achievement when they reach the appointed place – and the thought of a reward for getting there. Praise for their efforts – such as 'Well done Johnny, you're a real walker now' – also never goes amiss and instils a sense of pride in the youngster.

Strolling

Strolling can be enjoyed by families and individual adults alike, and is really walking without a set objective, such as a stroll around the park, by the riverside or along the coast.

This is probably the most relaxing form of walking, with no pressure to get anywhere in particular, giving you the time to really appreciate your surroundings and gain the maximum benefit from them.

The advent of the papoose for carrying young children has enabled young couples to take their children with them on walks.

WALKING WITH CHILDREN

Walking with children usually amounts to the parents or leaders rising to the challenge of constantly keeping their youngsters amused and interested. The physical act of walking to keep fit is unlikely to appeal to a child, so other ruses must be employed.

Walk guides know this principle very well. Frequent stops to point out places or things of interest are vitally important, and it is essential that the walk objective should not be too ambitious. The length of the walk should also be tailored to be able to be shortened at any point when, for reasons of waning interest or genuine tiredness, the kids have had enough.

School walking

Many children from non-walking families are introduced to the hobby on school field trips or holidays. While teachers have enormous responsibilities for the children's safety in such situations, and should on no account take chances, they can also be guilty of insisting on over-equipping their charges. Too often you see long crocodiles of school parties in the hills in hot summer weather, overburdened with huge frame rucksacks and clad in waterproof clothing, sweating their way along easy, low-level routes for which they are vastly over-equipped.

Many of these unfortunate children may be put off the hobby if they are led to believe that every walk requires such purgatory.

One of the greatest joys of walking with kids is sharing their wide-eyed sense of discovery, especially of the wildlife which can be encountered by the obser-

A toddler sets out on his first steps out of the papoose, hand-in-hand with Mum and Dad.

vant and sensitive guide, on walks in the countryside. This is one of the most rewarding aspects of the whole hobby of walking and, properly interpreted, can lead to a lifetime of pleasure for the participants whatever their age.

Many children receive their initial introduction to walking in the countryside through school field trips or organisations such as the Youth Hostels or the Scouting and Guiding movement.

Geography field trips or school holidays are often based in areas of high scenic beauty, and teachers will often involve their pupils in long walks into the countryside, sometimes instilling a love for the hobby which will last through to later life.

Youth hostels are often used for accommodation on such trips. They were originally set up in the early years of the 20th century by

A little encouragement is always a good thing, as this Mum is showing to her daughter on a long pull uphill.

a German teacher named Richard Schirrman, and his idea spread quickly through Europe and the rest of the world to become the international movement it is today. Originally designed to help young people of limited means enjoy the countryside, youth hostels are now open to all ages, and offer cheap, basic accommodation and meals. A stay usually involves the completion of a housekeeping 'task' before you leave. A comprehensive network of youth hostels now covers the world and there are hostels conveniently situated in most of the best walking areas.

The outdoor life is an important part of the ethos of Scouting and Guiding, international youth movements founded by British husband and wife Robert and Olave Baden-Powell in the early years of the 20th century. Scouting often involves camping trips and the learning of countryside skills, including backpacking and walking.

Ten tips for walking with kids

1. Be enthusiastic – it can be contagious
2. Don't walk too far
3. Avoid strenuous routes
4. Set your pace to that of the slowest walker
5. Find a route which has points of interest for kids
6. Set easily-attainable objectives
7. Praise or reward on reaching each objective
8. Stop often for rest or refreshment
9. Be prepared to stop your walk when children tire
10. Finally, always praise them at the end

GETTING READY

Time spent preparing for your walk is never time wasted. Good preparation and planning can mean the difference between an enjoyable experience and a disaster you'll never want to repeat. So before you set out, make sure you're fit and able to complete the planned walk, check your rights and read the guidebook. It's worth it.

FITNESS LEVELS AND TRAINING

Any reasonably fit person should be able to undertake a short walk without much in the way of special training. But if you are planning a longer walk, or perhaps one over more difficult terrain, it's a good idea to get yourself into shape first.

The way to do this is to embark on a walking programme that will fit in with your own lifestyle. The average person should aim to walk three times a week for at least 30 minutes at a brisk pace of between five and six kilometres per hour (3-4 miles per hour). This will strengthen your cardiovascular system, improve your endurance, tone your muscles and have the added benefit of burning off a few calories.

A good fitness regime – whatever your age – will soon get you walking effortlessly in situations like this, high on an Alpine path.

Warming up

Experts recommend that you should start your training walks slowly, and gradually build up to your best pace. This 'warming-up' session is important in order that extra strain is not placed on your vital organs too suddenly.

Some people recommend a few basic stretching exercises first, and these can certainly help in warming up your muscles. The muscles which need attention are the hamstrings, the calves, the front of the thighs, the shoulders and the muscles around the waist. It is important not to stretch cold muscles too vigorously, and not to jerk or strain them. You should ease into the stretching exercises slowly and smoothly to avoid pulling or straining your muscles. If stretching exercises are causing you any discomfort, you're doing them too hard or too fast.

The right rhythm

You should also practise breathing deeply and evenly, establishing a rhythm as you walk at a

Walking uphill is probably the easiest and most effective way to test your fitness, as this heavily-laden walker shows on a restored path in the mountains.

pace that you are completely comfortable with. This rhythm is vital on long-distance walks. When it is really working smoothly, you will find that it is often harder to stop, and have to start again and regain that rhythm, than it is just to keep walking.

When training, it is important to wear comfortable walking shoes and layered clothing, which can gradually be shed as you warm up. And if you are walking in town, you should take special care. The most dangerous part of a walking programme is stepping off the kerb to cross the road.

Finally, you should try to develop a good walking posture and a stride that feels natural and comfortable to you and achieves the desired pace. The back should be kept as straight as possible and the stomach held in, with the arms swinging freely and the elbows slightly bent.

Your personal pace – the number of steps you take per minute – will depend on your fitness, experience and target heart rate, and on the speed you need to achieve maximum aerobic benefit. You'll soon recognise your own personal steady rhythm.

PLANNING A WALK

For some people, it's enough just to get out for a walk. They stroll aimlessly with no objective or particular destination in mind. That type of walking was described on page 24, and for many people that's all they need or want. But for others, more enjoyment and satisfaction can be obtained by planning a walk carefully and setting certain targets, objectives or destinations before you set out.

The objective may be a simple one, such as attaining the summit of a hill or mountain, or walking between two villages or along a length of riverbank between two points. But whatever the objective, the more time taken planning your walk, the greater the satisfaction in completing it, attaining your objectives and getting back in time.

Think ahead

It is always worth getting out the map or the guidebook before you set out, deciding where you want to go and by which route, how long you aim to take and what you want to see en route. You can also plan in additional factors such as convenient refreshment stops to eat your sandwiches, places to have a picnic, or where to stop for a drink.

There may well be features of interest – for example an historic building or a natural feature such as a waterfall or lake – just off your route which you would like to make a short detour to see if time allows. All these things can add enormously to the pleasure of a walk, and should not be overlooked. And if you are relying on public transport, you will need to make an estimate of the time taken for the walk to be back in time to catch the bus or train home.

Naismith's rule

If you are walking through beautiful countryside, you will need to build in time for just stopping to admire the

Planning your route on the map before you set out is one of the pleasures of walking, as this young group is learning.

view or for taking a few photographs. Any hills en route will also take more time. Most people use Naismith's rule, which allows one hour for every five kilometres (3 miles), adding one hour for every 600 metres (2,000 ft) of ascent. Heavily-laden backpackers should allow one hour for every four kilometres (2½ miles), and an extra hour for every 450 metres (1,500 feet) of ascent. All this will add significantly to the total length of time taken for the walk.

Loops and relays

If you have your own transport, you will obviously want to get back to your starting point. This can be done by simply retracing the steps of your outward route, but it is much more satisfying and interesting to work out a circular route, returning by a different way from that of your outward journey. This obviously requires more planning and the use of the map to find an appropriate route back.

The ability to indentify features on the walk and relating them to the map will confirm your position quickly and accurately.

If you are in a party with two vehicles, you can adopt the relay system, which can be convenient as it avoids the retracing of steps on a linear walk. You leave one car at the destination of the walk, and then take everyone back to the starting point in the other. After you've done the walk, everyone gets in the first car which is driven back to the second at the start of the walk.

Great emphasis should be placed on constantly checking your route as you go, as this group is doing, so you know exactly where you are at any time.

It is always a good idea to keep your dog(s) on a lead in countryside especially where livestock might be grazing.

WALKERS' RIGHTS AND RESPONSIBILITIES

Although freedom from everyday restrictions is one of the major attractions of walking in the countryside, the walker is not entirely free from rights and responsibilities.

Where to walk

In cultivated countryside the walker must usually stick to rights-of-way – public footpaths, bridleways or byways. Footpaths are exclusively for the use of walkers – horse-riders and cyclists, are not allowed to use them. Footpaths are clearly marked on maps, and are often way-marked with colour-coded arrows.

Bridleways, sometimes way-marked in blue, are for walkers, horse riders or cyclists, while byways, which are usually former roads or roads now used as public paths, and public roads can be used by all wheeled traffic as well as walkers.

On rights-of-way you can also take a pram, pushchair or wheelchair, where practicable, and dogs on a lead or under close control, and you are allowed to take a short route around an illegal obstacle or remove it if it is blocking your way.

The UK

Under British law, a right-of-way is as much a part of the Queen's highway as a motorway, and the walker has exactly the same right to use it, freely and unhindered. It is just as illegal to block it as it would be to put up barricades on a motorway.

The law in Scotland and Ireland is slightly different, and there is a *de facto* right to walk anywhere in the open country of the hills and glens. During the 1990s, the British Government committed itself to a series of measures aimed at granting walkers the right to roam on all uncultivated country, mountains, moors and downland.

You may come across signs stating that 'Trespassers will be Prosecuted'. But because trespass is a civil wrong, and you must have damaged the landowner's property to be sued, you should not be intimidated.

North America

In the USA and Canada, where there is no local footpath network, there is a wealth of dedicated hiking trails. The most famous and best-used of these are the long-distance trails such as the Appalachian Trail, the Pacific Crest Trail and the Continental Divide Trail (see

page 18). There is also a
well-developed network of
way-marked trails in all the
popular National Parks of
North America.

A more recent develop-
ment in the USA has been
the 'Rails to Trails' Conser-
vancy, which aims to con-
vert former and now
disused railway tracks –
which were public rights of
way when in use – into
walking routes. With a total
of over 400,000 kilometres
(250,000 miles) of railway
track, the potential of these
routes is enormous.

Responsibilities

In addition to the rights
mentioned above, the
walker has certain responsibilities when using the
countryside. In Britain, this
has been distilled into what
is known as the Country
Code – which, in simple
terms, states that you
should respect the life and
work of the countryside. The
US National Parks Service
has encapsulated this suc-
cinctly into the maxim:
'Take nothing but photo-
graphs. Leave nothing but
footprints.'

**When a right of way crosses a
field boundary the owner is duty-
bound to provide a stile.**

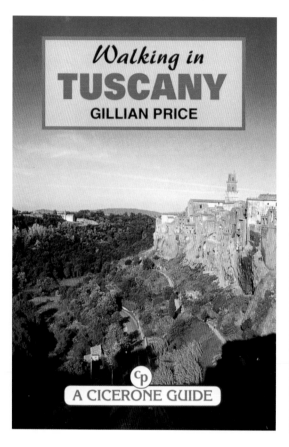

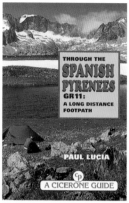

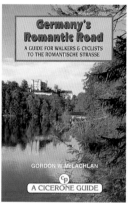

GUIDEBOOKS

A good guidebook can turn a good walk into a great one. And spending time studying it before you set out will ensure that you know the way, and that you enjoy points of interest along the route which you might otherwise miss.

The best guidebooks have clear, easy-to-follow directions, plenty of interpretation and descriptions of places and things of interest along the route, and scaled sketch maps giving you a fair idea of the kind of terrain which can be expected on the walk. Some guidebooks use licensed extracts from the relevant maps. The most practical guidebooks are the portable ones, which slip inside your pocket or rucksack. A glossy, coffee-table guide is of little use in the field.

The key facts

A 'fact box' will summarise the walk in terms of start and finish points, with map references, length of the walk, average time for completion, degree of difficulty, and the appropriate maps which cover the walk. In these days of sustainable hiking, the fact box should also give details of public transport connections, enabling walkers to leave their cars at home.

Although the guidebook sketch map should give a an accurate representation of the walk, it will rarely

It's worth investing in a good guidebook if you are walking in unfamiliar territory, such as this range from Cicerone.

replace relevant maps which can carry so much more detail than any sketch map ever can. They also extend the area covered around the walk, which is useful when detours are planned, or if you are unfortunate enough to get lost and stray from the directed route.

Other information

Under the heading of 'interpretation of the walk', the

A guidebook will tell you much more than a map about what there is to see on the walk, so occasionally take the time to check it out.

best guidebooks explain the underlying geology, landscape features, natural history and wildlife that the walker might expect to see while out on the walk. In addition, any items of historical interest, anecdotes and folklore associated with the route and its environs will be described, making the walk a true exploration, with points of interest at every step. Some guidebooks have very specific themes – for example, woodland walks, riverside walks, birdwatching walks or hill or mountain walking.

Guidebooks to long-distance routes, National Trails or general areas will usually give details of accommodation and useful addresses including those of the relevant tourist boards and information and visitor centres.

Finally, the best guidebooks also have good quality illustrations taken from the walk. These can be either photographs or line drawings, which will give potential users a good idea of the kind of scenery and highlights they can expect to see on the route.

Wainwright Guides

The only exception to the general rule that sketch maps are inferior to conventional maps is the work of the late Alfred Wainwright. His series of seven classic hand-scripted *Pictorial Guides* to England's Lakeland Fells were published between 1952 and 1965. The author lovingly created three-dimensional maps of such clarity and detail of all the major Lake District hills in the north west of England, that the relevant OS maps were almost made redundant. Every conceivable detour and alternative route was included in these masterpieces of the guidebook writers' art, but unfortunately they were never revised by the author, and many are badly out of date today.

EQUIPMENT: WHAT TO WEAR

Well-equipped walkers have nothing to fear from the weather. Come wind or rain, they will be cocooned in a windproof and waterproof shell, enabling them to actually enjoy the worst that the elements can throw at them. Well-shod in sturdy, waterproof boots or shoes, they can stride out over the most difficult terrain without a care.

BOOTS AND SHOES

The single most important item of equipment you need to buy before you set out walking is your footwear. A good, well-fitting pair of boots or shoes is the key to comfortable walking, so it's worth spending a little time on choosing a pair that both do the job and fit you perfectly.

First of all, you need to decide what kind of walking you will be doing. Will it be mainly urban or fitness walking in town, or will it be lowland or family strolling in the countryside? Maybe your aim is to head for the hills, where conditions underfoot can be much more testing. Whatever you decide, it's essential to buy the right boots.

Sturdy Boots

Most country walkers, lowland or upland, swear by a good sturdy pair of boots which will give ankle support, dry feet and a good foothold when walking over any kind of rough country. Traditionally, walking boots were made of heavy leather with Vibram and sometimes even nailed soles. During a long day's walking, these boots could significantly add to the fatigue of the walker.

Modern footwear

Today's most popular boots are lightweight, weighing no

Lightweight boots such as these are now the most popular form of walkers' footwear.

more than a few pounds, and can be made of either leather or a breathable fabric, such as Gore-Tex. Leather is still most walkers' preference because it is comfortable, durable and more waterproof than fabric. Most boots are made with a one-piece upper, thus avoiding seams which can let in the water, and have a sturdy 'rand' where the upper joins the sole, a padded cuff around the ankle, and a bellows-type tongue which is designed to stop water seeping in. The boots are secured by strong laces which tie through D rings and hooks for ease of lacing and a better-fitting instep.

Mountain boots are stronger and more rigid, and generally have higher ankle support. They will also have fittings for crampons – spiked steel frames which are attached to the sole to improve grip in ice or snow.

Fabric boots are usually made of a nylon material with suede leather panels reinforce those parts of the boot most prone to wear.

They became popular because of their lightness, ease of fitting and breathability, but were never quite as waterproof or durable as leather boots, even with the insertion of waterproof membranes.

Good walking trail shoes can give as much support as a lightweight boot, and many women prefer them. A recent innovation has been the sports sandal which, in summer conditions, is much cooler and lighter than boots or shoes and gives as good a grip.

In the shop

When buying boots, it is a good idea to have your feet measured in a specialist shop. Your shoe size is not necessarily your ideal boot size. Try the boots on wearing heavy walking socks, and make sure that they fit snugly with no movement of the foot inside the boot. This is how blisters are caused. Strange as it may seem, it's a good idea to try on your new boots in the afternoon – your feet expand during the day, and boots which are comfortable in the morning may be too tight later on. Try several pairs so that you can compare the fit and weight of each.

Heavyweight trainers like these are suitable for summer walking in dry conditions, but should not be used in winter.

Sturdy walking shoes like these are a popular alternative to the boot. While they do not support the ankle they are perfectly suitable for lowland walking.

Sports sandals are becoming increasingly popular for summer walking, when their lightness and coolness can be an advantage over boots.

Getting a good fit is vital with any walking footwear, so make sure you have your feet measured properly before you purchase.

Ten tips when buying boots

1. Decide what kind of boot you want – is it for lowland or hill-walking?
2. Do you want leather or fabric boots, shoes or sandals?
3. Get your feet measured in the shop
4. Wear walking socks when you try the boots on
5. Make sure you have the right width boot for your feet
6. Check you get the lacing right
7. Check the fit carefully by walking around the shop
8. Find out if you need an absorbent footbed inside the boot
9. Ask about boot care and protection
10. Break in the boots gradually

UNDERWEAR AND SOCKS

It is very important to keep your body and feet warm and dry when out walking, especially if you are venturing into the hills. Being cold and wet through can easily lead to hypothermia or exposure, and most walkers adopt the 'layering' system to avoid such dangers.

Wearing several thin layers of clothing is generally better than having one thick one because you can adjust your clothing to suit the weather and conditions as you walk.

The base layer

The layering system starts with your underclothing, or the base layer. This should remove moisture or sweat from your skin as quickly as possible so that your sweat does not stay next to your body, cool and eventually make you colder. Base layer fabrics can be synthetic or natural. The key requirements are that they take the moisture away from your skin (the technical term is 'wicking') and that they dry very quickly when they get wet. Lightweight

Good woollen socks with reinforced toes and heels will make your feet feel comfortable inside your boots however far you walk.

fabrics are best for strenuous walking, climbing or scrambling, whereas heavier ones are much more suitable for winter conditions. If you prefer natural materials next to your skin, silk and wool alternatives can work just as well.

A good base layer of underwear should perform like a second skin, keeping

and they can minimise the friction caused by the movement of your feet inside the boots. They are therefore very important items of any hiker's equipment, and should never be underestimated.

The fabric which performs all these functions more efficiently than any other is a natural one: wool. Cotton and synthetic socks may be adequate for summer strolling, but all too often they soak up water like a sponge and take a very long time to dry out, making your feet cold in the process. Wool socks will avoid this problem – they are also extremely comfortable, providing excellent cushioning.

So with a sound base layer which will make both your feet and body feel comfortable, you should be prepared for anything the weather can throw at you.

your own skin at the optimum temperature and helping you feel fresh, warm and dry all day.

When you are trying on a new pair of boots, you should also wear a pair of walking socks to get the best fit.

Socks

Heavy woollen socks are often portrayed, along with heavy boots, as the trademark of the hardy rambler, but the simple fact is that they do the job better than anything else. Socks serve four basic purposes: they cushion your feet inside the boots; they keep your feet warm and dry; they absorb the sweat from your feet;

JACKETS

Probably the most important single layer garment is the jacket, which, if it's doing its job properly, should do three things. It should keep you warm, windproof and waterproof. There is a tremendous range of modern outdoor jackets in a multitude of colours, styles and prices. Again, you should always buy according to your personal requirements. There is little point in buying an expensive, Everest-specification jacket if you are only going to use it on country hikes.

Clothes that breath

Old-fashioned waxed and waterproof jackets were made of synthetic materials which, although they kept the rain out, made you just as wet on the inside whenever you did any strenuous, sweat-inducing exercise such as walking uphill. The great advantage of modern fabrics, such as Gore-Tex, is that they are breathable. That means they keep the wind and rain out while allowing moisture from your body to escape through tiny micropores in the fabric, which are too small to allow the rain in. However, it must be said that no jacket is going to be entirely condensation-free, so you must expect a little dampness when you are exerting yourself on a hill or mountain climb. A good jacket will have a knitted mesh lining for comfort.

Insulated jackets such as this may be fashion items, but for the walker they are only suitable for the coldest of winter conditions.

Rain resistance

The weakest point on any waterproof garment is the seams, and you should try to buy a jacket where all the seams are sealed. Another important requirement is a hood, which should be big enough to cover a hat as well. People who wear spectacles should ensure that the hood has a wired peak which will stop the rain obscuring their lenses. Drawcords are used to pull the hood tightly around the face in heavy rain or blizzard conditions.

Ventilation and pockets

Ventilation is important in an outdoor jacket. Look for a strong zip up the front, which can be covered by a 'storm flap' to keep the rain out. Some modern jackets also have armpit zips, which also improve ventilation. Cuffs should be adjustable – usually via Velcro fastening – for the same reason.

Pockets are vital in a jacket. They provide somewhere to put your gloves and hat and are useful for keeping your hands warm. They should all have a wide flap to keep the rain out. One of the most important pockets

Above: A good wired hood is essential on your waterproof jacket, especially if you are walking in a wet climate such as that in Britain.

Left: A walking jacket can never have enough pockets, as these high-performance jackets in breathable, waterproof fabric show.

is the map pocket, which should be big enough to take a standard sheet map.

You can also buy simple, unlined waterproof jackets – usually known as cagoules – which are simply waterproofs, and in which condensation is always going to be a problem for the active walker. At the other end of the scale are the insulated jackets worn by mountaineers which are filled with synthetic or feather-based down, and are really only suitable for the coldest of winter conditions.

TROUSERS AND BREECHES

With the top half of your body protected by a good jacket, you now need to worry about the bottom half – and that means trousers or breeches.

There is one thing that is vitally important to emphasise if you are going to take up serious walking, and that is the 'no-jeans' rule. Although denim may be perfectly all right in good weather conditions, it must be avoided if there is a chance of wind or rain. Wet, jeans become unbelievably heavy and very, very cold to the skin, soon causing shivering and, at worst, hypothermia. They also take an age to dry out, when and if the sun appears.

No jeans

If you are used to wearing jeans and then try a pair of proper walking trousers or breeches for the first time, you won't believe the difference. You'll notice how light they are, and you'll notice the greater freedom of movement, but most importantly you'll appreciate the improved performance in wind- and waterproofing.

Most walkers these days plump for synthetic, poly-cotton or cotton full-length trousers. The advantage of synthetic trousers is that

Many walkers prefer lightweight polycotton trousers with plenty of zipped pockets and a good waistbelt, like these.

For the serious winter walker these mountaineering trousers provide excellent durability and comfort with reinforcements and a fleece interior.

Shorts give the walker a great sense of freedom and are the standard legwear for many walkers in summer.

they absorb less moisture and will dry out much quicker than cotton or poly-cotton ones. The better walking trousers are made from wind- and water-resistant material, and have reinforced knees and seat. Quality trousers also have plenty of zipped pockets, including one large enough to take a map.

Some people prefer stretch-nylon or polyester tracksuit bottoms for walking, and they certainly give you comfort and more freedom of movement than ordinary trousers.

Shorts

In summer conditions, however, nothing is better than a good pair of shorts, which in addition to giving you freedom of movement and keeping you much cooler than trousers, give you the chance to give those legs a tan! But a word of warning; beware the brambles.

Old-fashioned breeches

Many old-fashioned walkers still swear by their breeches – the trousers which end at calf level on the leg where they are fastened by a Velcro fixing or buttons over a knee-length sock. The argument is that they give greater leg freedom for the walker, with no uncomfortable brushing against vegetation as you march through the long grass or heather.

As with all types of clothing, you will only get what you are prepared to pay for with trousers, shorts or breeches. It is usually worth paying a little bit more to get yourself kitted out in clothing which will both perform well in the field and give a lifetime's use if looked after properly.

GAITERS AND OVERTROUSERS

There's nothing worse than the feeling of having wet feet or legs on a walk. It is obviously uncomfortable and the cold it causes can sap your strength if conditions don't improve and you get no chance to dry out. Many walkers swear by gaiters or over-trousers, which are made of water-repellent materials such as PVC or Gore-tex.

Gaiters are particularly effective in keeping snow or mud out of your boots in winter conditions.

Traditional gaitors

Gaiters are waterproofed tube-like fabric coverings which protect the lower leg and boot to just below the knee. They were originally designed for use in the high mountains to keep snow out of boots, and they are obviously very effective in winter conditions. They are also equally useful in protecting the boots, socks and trousers from muddy or boggy conditions, loose stones, grass seeds or heather. They will help to keep your feet and lower legs dry and warm, doing away with the gap between boot and trousers.

The traditional gaitor is fastened to the lower end of the boot laces with a hook, and has a strap which passes under the instep to stop it riding up. The upper and lower parts of the gaiter and the ankle are usually elasticated so that it fits closely over the leg and the top of the boot.

Yetis

A more recent innovation has been the all-over gaiter – the so-called 'supergaiter' or 'Yeti' type, which covers the whole boot. These are fixed by a thick rubber rand which grips tightly around the base of the boot and a wide band which passes under the instep. They are zipped at the front to make them easy to get on and off, an operation which is notoriously difficult. Many serious walkers finding themselves in situations where they need protection for several days will leave their Yetis in place when they remove their boots.

Yeti-type gaiters do not fit all boots, so make sure they fit yours before you purchase them. Also, the rubber rands and base band are easily damaged when walking over rough, rocky ground. Despite these negatives, yetis are an excellent form of lower leg and boot protection.

Left: Overtrousers should have knee-length zips at the side like these, to allow them to slip easily over the boots.

Right: Good overtrousers should also have an adjustable drawcord at the waist, to stop them slipping down when walking.

Below: Overtrousers are light and easily folded allowing them to be carried in a backpack when not required.

Complete leg protection

Waterproof overtrousers fit completely over your normal trousers, and are essential in prolonged heavy rainfall. You often see walkers putting on and taking off their overtrousers between showers, but in such weather it's really not worth the effort required. Overtrousers are usually quite uncomfortable items of clothing; they are noisy and make your legs sweat, so they should only be used in extremely wet conditions.

They should have an adjustable waist drawcord, to stop them slowly slipping down, and the best models also have knee-length zips at the side to allow them to fit easily over boots. Some models have full-length side zips, which can be opened up to improve ventilation of the legs and prevent the problem of sweating.

The end of the 1990s saw the fleece make the transition from highly practical outdoor clothing to a desirable fashion item.

FLEECES

The real revolution in outdoor clothing in recent years has been the advent of fleece for what is known as the mid-layer – the layer between the base and the outer, water- and windproof shell.

Traditionally, the mid-layer has consisted of items such as woollen sweaters or cotton sweatshirts, and while wool is still the best insulator, cotton sweatshirts are heavy and soak up moisture very quickly, making them even heavier and colder. Most walkers will carry an extra woollen sweater in the rucksack, just in case it turns colder on a walk.

Perfect layer

Fleece is light and warm, and it is perfect for the 'layering' system, mentioned on page 42. Several thin layers are much better, and hold more warm air between them, than one heavy layer. And several layers are much easier to adjust to the prevailing conditions than one.

Practical and fashionable

Fleece is fashionable and it has a lot to offer. Usually made of a polyester material such as Polartec, fleece has the triple advantages of

being warm, lightweight and very comfortable to wear. It is also quick drying and hard-wearing.

You can get different weights of fleece, in a bewildering multitude of 'colourways', to suit your needs. You can even get 'green' alternative fleeces made from recycled plastic bottles. The heavier fleece jackets are also windproof and have a lining made from a thin, windproof material or have a windproof membrane between two layers of fleece which achieves the same result. This type of

Right: A two-tone walkers' fleece with zipped pockets and a draw-cord at the waist should keep you snug and warm in colder conditions.

Above: This heavy-duty fleece would be more suitable for winter, or three-season use and would probably be too warm for the summer.

Right: Thermal shirts such as this example can be used as a jacket, providing you have an adequate shirt or vest beneath.

jacket also serves perfectly well as an outer, shell-type layer garment in all but the worst kinds of weather.

There are three basic thicknesses of fleece material, and you need to choose the one that will suit the conditions you are most likely to meet on your regular walking expeditions. Obviously, the heavier the material, the warmer the garment, and lightweight fleeces are therefore ideal for summer use and heavy ones for the coldest days in winter.

All fleeces transport perspiration away from the body while keeping you warm, and some are treated with a durable, water-repellent finish which makes them virtually shower-proof too, thus dispensing with the need for a separate outer rain jacket in most conditions.

Good-sized, weather-proof zipped pockets are important in a serviceable fleece jacket. Not only are they good to keep things (such as a map) in – they can also keep your hands warm in cold weather without having to bother with gloves.

Again, the better-quality fleeces tend to be the most expensive, but you'll find that a good fleece jacket is such an adaptable and comfortable garment that you won't want to take it off.

HEADGEAR AND HEAD TORCHES

The cartoonist's image of a rambler usually shows him or her wearing the apparently compulsory woolly bobble hat. This unfashionable and rather quaint item of clothing may have become something of a trademark of the walker, but the importance of good, warm headgear, especially in winter, cannot be overestimated.

Keep the heat in

It's a common saying among walkers that if you've got cold feet and hands, you should wear a hat and, strange as it may seem, it is true. In cold conditions, your body automatically slows down the blood supply to the extremities first, so that the vital organs in the core of the body and the head can be properly supplied and protected. This is often the root cause of frostbite in the hands and toes. It's also said that up to 90 per cent of heat loss is through the head – so in cold conditions, it is vital to keep your head covered. If you do, you may be

Below: Fleece hats like these have become quite fashionable, and they are excellent head-warmers for the walker.

Above: Balaclavas are really only suitable for extreme winter conditions.

REGATTA
GREAT OUTDOORS

REGATTA

REGATTA
GREAT OUTDOORS

surprised to notice that you very quickly begin to feel warmer all over.

Types of hat

What headgear should you wear? Well, there's still a lot to be said for that traditional woolly hat, which has the advantage that it can be pulled down over your ears if it gets really cold. Some woolly hats actually transform into a Balaclava, covering the whole of the ears and neck, for really severe weather conditions.

There are many other types of hats on the market which will keep your head warm. But the best all have built-in flaps which fold down to keep your ears warm when the temperature starts to plummet.

Summer hats

A hat will not only protect you against the cold, it will also protect you against the heat of the sun. A hat with a wide brim or peak keeps the sun out of your eyes, and it will also keep your head cool and avoid sunburn on the face and neck. Current concerns about the dangers of skin cancer make a hat a sensible precaution to take in high summer.

There are many types of summer-weight hat which can fulfil this role, from the common-or-garden baseball cap to the specialist wide-brimmed sunhat, as worn by intrepid explorers. The best hats all have wide brims to keep off both the sun and the rain, do not shrink or go soggy when they get wet, and have good ventilation characteristics. Most are made from cotton, which in this case is the most effective material because it is absorbent, slow-drying and, above all, cool.

Lighting up

While on the subject of headgear, packing a head torch in the rucksack is a good idea in case you find yourself out in the dark at the end of a walk. This is simply a battery-operated torch that straps around the head and allows the hands to be free for map-reading or compass work, which becomes especially important if you are in danger of becoming benighted on a hill walk. You should also carry spare batteries whenever possible.

Above: A headtorch has the dual advantages of freeing your hands for map and compass work while lighting the path ahead.

Left: A wide-brimmed hat keeps the sun out of your eyes and also keeps your head cool avoiding sunburn on the face and neck.

EQUIPMENT: WHAT TO CARRY

Sooner or later, you will have to think about a rucksack for carrying essential equipment, extra clothing or food and drink as your walks get longer and more ambitious. You will also need to choose between a simple day sack, or a larger backpack if you plan on camping. And if you have a young child, then a papoose is an absolute must.

DAY SACKS

The sense of freedom provided by a simple rucksack to carry your gear for a day's walking has to be experienced to be believed. You become a self-contained, self-sufficient walker for the first time, ready and confident to face any eventuality.

Your first day sack does not need to be anything too sophisticated. It just needs to be large enough to carry extra clothing and waterproofs, your lunch and a drink, and to have enough pockets for small objects such as a map and compass.

The basic bag

Rucksacks are sized by their capacity, and a day sack needs to be no more than 20 to 50 litres in size. The design of such sacks is usually fairly basic, ranging from the simplest, consisting of a bag with a drawcord to seal it at the top and perhaps a map pocket in the 'lid', to ones which bristle with special features and pockets. For most walkers, certainly for beginners, the simple bag type is probably all that's needed. In all cases, however, broad and well-padded shoulder straps are vital.

Key features

The more sophisticated rucksacks have zipped pockets built into the sides

Above and left: A simple day sack should accommodate all your needs for a day's walking, with plenty of pockets and good shoulder straps.

which are useful for carrying smaller objects such as your camera or compass. There are often special map pockets, and there is usually a zipped pocket in the lid which is handy for this type of thing. The lid is fastened by straps which can be tightened and secured to the bottom of the sack by strong, plastic clips. There are also straps to which you can fasten your trekking poles or, for winter use in the hills, your ice axe.

The best sacks have a waist belt and chest straps which help to stop the rucksack moving about. Padded backs and some kind of meshed ventilation system between the sack and your back are other good features to look out for, and should help stop perspiration when in use.

Most rucksacks are made from lightweight material such as nylon or polyester and, though many are in theory waterproof, they are often let down by gaps created by the stitching of the seams. The best sacks are made from coated material and have welded seams which will keep out

even the heaviest downpour. With cheaper rucksacks it's often a good idea to use a waterproof liner inside the sack. Specially-made ones are available, but any reasonably thick plastic bag, such as a refuse bag, will do.

Try it first

It is important to try on your rucksack and make sure it is comfortable before you decide to buy it. If you can, try it loaded with some weight, as most rucksacks will feel quite comfortable when empty. And choose one which fits your height, too. For example, if you are tall and have a long back, a short rucksack can be very uncomfortable, especially after a long day's walking.

Top: A larger, 50-litre day sack, suitable for longer, more serious expeditions, with extra pockets and more sophisticated features.

Bottom: The ubiquitous 'bum bag' (left) is favoured by some walkers for carrying their valuables, and the 'collar safe' (right) is another solution to the same problem.

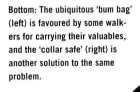

BACKPACKS

The backpack is the walkers' equivalent of the motorists' caravan. These large, internally-framed rucksacks are used to carry everything the walker/camper needs on his or her back on longer, multi-day trips into the wilds.

They are the easiest and most comfortable method of transporting your equipment and provisions with you, and modern backpacks are masterpieces of ergonomic design. They are often subjected to rigorous testing, sometimes on large-scale mountaineering expeditions to some of the highest mountain ranges in the world.

Pockets and padding

Backpacks, which are usually over 50 litres and can be up to 90 litres in capacity, have several additional features over the day sack, apart from their obviously greater size. They have a broad and well-padded shoulder harness as well as shoulder straps, a very broad and well-padded hip belt with a back support pad, and often an adjustable back support system built into the construction of the sack. All these features help to transfer the weight of the sack from the shoulders to the

Packing your rucksack properly is a key skill. The basic rule here is 'first in, last out'.

padded hip belt which is sewn directly into the base of the rucksack. This brings the weight of the loaded rucksack much closer to the back, and has the added advantage of improving stability. Again, the sack should be tried on in the shop, preferably loaded, to ensure a good fit in relation to height and size.

The hip belt transfers the weight to the pelvis and down through the thighs. All these measures have the

Far left: Handy side-pockets mark this rucksack as suitable for longer expeditions. Note the strap for carrying an ice axe on the back.

Left: A larger, 70-litre rucksack, suitable for more serious back-packing expeditions.

Below: A 60-litre capacity ruck-sack is ideal for expeditions lasting a couple of days.

important effect of shifting weight away from the spinal column and shoulders to stronger areas of the body. Many backpacks also have a sternum strap across the chest, which limits movement of the sack while loaded and in use, and haulage straps at the top of the sack which can be used to strap on sleeping bags outside the sack itself.

Many of these larger rucksacks now have a split compartment about two-thirds of the way down the main body of the sack, which enables you to gain access to the contents of the bottom of the sack without having to unpack the items at the top.

These internally-framed rucksacks are ideal for multi-day expeditions and long-distance path walking tours, although it is a useful tip to check if there is a rucksack carrying service on popular routes, such as the Pennine Way and Appalachian Trail.

Remember, however waterproof the pack is, water can enter through seams and zippers so a cover or extra lining is advisable.

Packing

Learning how to pack your rucksack is important, and discipline here will be repaid when you have to unpack to set up camp, perhaps in adverse weather conditions.

Most people like to keep their stove and fuel in the bottom of the sack, with spare clothing and food above that and the tent and waterproofs nearer to the top of the sack, where they can be accessed quickly and easily. The principle of 'first in, last out' applies when packing your ruck-sack, as always.

PAPOOSES

When children arrive in a family which enjoys walking, the problem arises of how to bring the kids along before they can walk very far themselves. The normal pushchair is pretty useless out in the country, although recently more rugged, foldable three-wheeled models have come onto the market.

Native American design

The best way for a young child to enjoy a country walk is from the safety of a specially-designed papoose. Based on carrying devices used by nomadic Native Americans, the modern papoose is basically an adapted rucksack which enables the child to be carried on an adult's back.

Children are surprisingly adaptable, and although many papooses may look fairly uncomfortable at first sight, children quickly get used to them, and often fall

The height and close proximity to the adult means that children generally enjoy riding on their parents' back in a papoose.

asleep after the first mile or so, despite, or perhaps because of, the constant rocking motion.

Choosing a carrier

There are several kinds of child-carriers for walkers. The simplest form is just an externally-framed rucksack without a covering 'lid' and with holes in the sides for the child's legs to poke through and hang behind the arms of the carrier. The problem with this type is that it does not give good back or neck support to the child, whose head will loll from side to side when he or she gets sleepy. Others have a canopy-type cover which shields the child from the wind and rain.

Another type of papoose allows the child to sit in an integral seat, with his or her legs hanging down against the carrier. Some models also incorporate a foot rest. The child's back is supported by a firm framework.

In each case, the child sits in the papoose with his or her face pointing in the direction of travel, and getting a grandstand view of what's going on around. Most children seem to enjoy this experience, usually preferring to be carried rather than walking in any case.

A traditional, fixed frame child papoose or child carrier, in which the youngster sits in the harness, looking forward.

A more sophisticated child carrier with back support and strapping, suitable for younger children or babies.

Clothing for your passenger

Despite the fact that they are encased in the papoose, it is important to remember that the child should be adequately dressed for the outdoors as well. This means warm, water- and windproof clothing and headgear. Hats are particularly important in the winter because of the heat loss which is experienced through the head, and also in summer because of the danger of sunstroke on young, unprotected heads.

TREKKING POLES

It's said that after an eight-hour walk in the hills, the average walker will have carried a weight equivalent to 62 full-grown African bush elephants. Research at the University of Salzburg and in the English Lake District has discovered that using two trekking poles can give an average relief per step of about eight kilogrammes (17½ pounds).

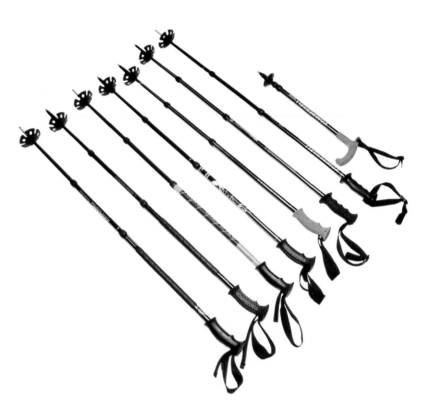

Spread the load

That means that during an eight-hour walk, the use of a pair of poles will relieve the strain on your hips and knee joints by a massive 250 tonnes – or the equivalent of those 62 elephants.

Trekking poles were first used by guides in the European Alps, and the long-stick variety was much favoured by 18th century alpinists all over the world. The modern, shorter, high-tech versions have recently become very popular with hill-walkers in Britain and America.

Why use poles?

Apart from the welcome relief provided by the transfer of that enormous amount of weight from the hips, knees and lower back, trekking poles can significantly increase the walker's stability on rough ground. They provide two extra points of contact with the ground – in effect giving you four legs instead of two. And they allow much faster

The range of trekking poles now available is bewildering, as this display shows. Choose ones which fit your height.

movement over difficult terrain, especially when travelling steeply up or down hill. They can also be invaluable when crossing swollen streams or rivers, or when traversing slippery grass or snowy slopes. Those extra points of contact with the ground can increase the walker's confidence enormously, thus encouraging him or her to take on more difficult terrain.

Trekking poles allow the whole body to be used when walking, bringing the arms and the upper body into use in addition to the legs and lower body. This extra support is said to exercise the upper body and allow the walker to travel the same distance on less energy, or further on exactly the same amount of energy expended.

Modern poles

Modern trekking poles are usually made of lightweight aluminium and have integrated anti-shock systems – usually pressurised springs – built into their design. Their telescopic shafts can be adjusted to suit the individual walker's most comfortable height, but if you are tall make sure you buy a pole which is long enough. Telescopic poles can be strapped to your rucksack when they are not required. They also have strong, tungsten carbide tips and circular stone, mud or snow 'baskets' protecting the end of the pole. Most have a firm, easy-grip shaped handle with a strap which winds around the wearer's wrist for security.

Some walkers use a single pole, but most prefer the better balance achieved by the use of a pair. This is most noticeable when the walker is carrying a heavy backpack, when the weight-reducing qualities of the poles are especially evident.

Trekking poles have recently enjoyed a huge surge of popularity among hill-walkers, and many users swear by their weight- and strain-reducing abilities.

Above: A couple stride out happily into the mountains, aided by their trekking poles.

Right: Two poles are better than one, especially on steep or uneven ground such as that faced by this walker.

FINDING YOUR WAY

Getting lost is no joke when you are starting out on your walking career, but as the great walking and access campaigner G.H.B. 'Bert' Ward used to say: 'The man who never was lost, never went very far.' The secret of good navigation is understanding your map and knowing how to use your compass and, more recently, your GPS equipment.

MAP READING

Maps are the key to understanding and enjoying the countryside. With just a little practice, they can be read like a book and can tell readers much of what they can expect to see on their walk.

Maps should be used first to plan your walk, then as a navigational aid when you are on the walk, and finally to reflect on where you've been when you get back home. It's a good idea, especially in bad weather, to carry your map in a transparent plastic map case, which can be slung around your neck.

In Britain, the most popular and most detailed maps are produced by the Ordnance Survey – Britain's national mapping agency – although there are others who produce excellent walkers' maps, such as Harveys Maps of Doune, Perthshire.

Scales and other details

The most common scale of OS map is the 1:50,000 (about 1.25 inches to the mile) Landranger series, which shows public footpaths and bridleways and all major historical and geographical features. Better still for walkers is the 1:25,000 scale (about 2.5 inches to the mile) Pathfinder or Explorer series, which is even more detailed and shows not only all the rights of way but also field boundaries. The Outdoor Leisure Maps (OLMs) are at the same scale and cover most National Parks, Areas of Outstanding Natural Beauty and popular tourist destinations. Useful information for the visitor, such as sites and long-distance and leisure walking routes, are also shown on all these maps.

Ordnance Survey maps also show contour lines (lines of equal height above sea level) which, with a little experience, will indicate hills, valleys and plains to the walker. The unique OS Nat-

A selection of Ordnance Survey 1:50,000 Landranger maps, with a waterproof mapholder for carrying around the neck.

ional Grid system also allows you to trace with a fair degree of accuracy any particular point on the map, say the start or finish point of a walk.

Such large scale and detailed maps are uncommon in other countries, and most walkers' maps are produced at the 1:50,000 scale. Particularly good is the Swiss National Map Survey, the Eidgenoecssische Landestopographie, whose maps show footpaths and cover the whole country at scales of 1:100,000, 1:50,000 and 1:25,000. In France the Carte de France publish maps at 1:50,000 and 1:25,000 which show footpaths, and although there is no official national mapping agency in Germany, Topographische Karte surveys are available for most states. The Wanderwegausgabe editions at 1:50,000 and 1:25,000 both show footpaths. Maps suitable for walkers are more difficult to find in the USA, although in popular areas, outdoor shops and tourist offices will stock local maps.

But in all popular walking areas there will be leaflets and guidebooks giving sketch maps of the most

It is important that all members of your party can read and understand the map and know where you are, in case of emergency.

popular walks, which will also probably be way-marked to aid navigation.

Using maps

Understanding the key is absolutely crucial to map reading, and, with a little experience, you'll soon get to know what all the symbols on the map mean, and be able to find your way across country with ease. Being able to use your map in association with your compass (which we will be looking at next) is an important skill, especially if you are walking in the hills or in featureless country, or if you find yourself in bad weather conditions.

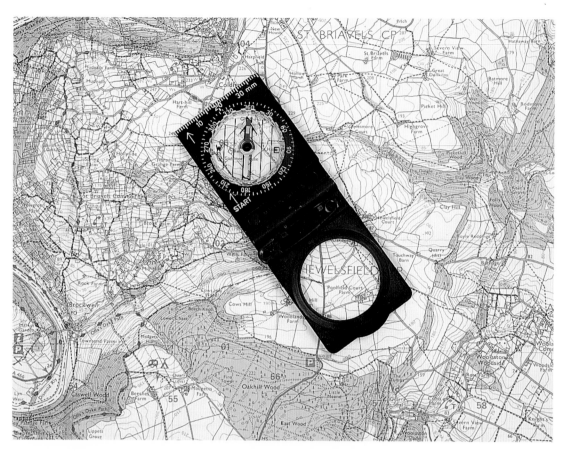

USING A COMPASS

It's thought that it was the Chinese who were the first to discover (about 4,500 years ago) that when a lodestone was floated on a piece of wood in water and allowed to rotate freely, it would always point in the same direction. This simple experiment, later used by Arabs and Vikings, is still the principle of the compass – surely the greatest single invention in the history of navigation.

Base plate or sighting compass

Walkers use two main types of compass – the base plate compass and the sighting compass. Of these it is the base plate type which is by far the most common. It consists of a flat, transparent plastic base plate with a compass in a sealed capsule on top. The base plate will have various maps scales engraved on it, to be used in conjunction with the map and the direction of travel arrow. Sometimes a magnifying glass is incorporated into the base plate to help read the map.

Sighting compasses are more accurate than the base plate type, and have to be held up to the eye of the user and looked through or across using reference lines to line up the object. They are, however, much more expensive and difficult to use and can only be used in good weather.

A good compass will also have a 'romer' scale, which is used to work out an exact, six-figure grid reference from an OS map, and a cord attached so that it can be slung around your neck when not in use.

The key to navigation is being able to relate the map to the compass, or 'setting' the map, which involves aligning the north-south grid lines on the map to the north arrow on the compass.

How to use it

The easiest way of using the base plate compass with your map is to place the compass on the map flat in front of you and then turn your body until the north arrow on the compass points in the same direction as the north grid lines on the map. Then when you look up, you should be able to identify the features shown on the

Constant reference to map and compass should ensure you do not get lost and always know approximately where you are. It's always worth stopping and checking if you are unsure of your position, certainly before you go too far off route.

map with the actual view on the ground in front of you, and decide in which direction you need to travel.

All compasses used in the northern hemisphere point to magnetic north; however, you should be aware that confusingly there are three norths marked on OS maps. These are: true north (the actual north pole); the magnetic north, to which the compass always points but which changes slightly from year to year (check your map); and grid north, the north shown by the grid lines on the map.

By adding or subtracting the declination from grid north (found in the key of all OS maps), you will be able to head in precisely the right direction, although for most lowland walks this would not be necessary.

You can use your compass to check from the map to the compass for your required direction, or to check from your compass to your map to find out exactly where you are, identify a feature or work out the aspect of a slope to help find your position – especially in bad weather.

Three steps to finding your way

There are three simple steps to plot a course from the map to the compass.
After deciding precisely where you are and where you want to go:
1. Place the edge of the compass on the map so that it connects your current position with where you want to go (so that the whole compass points in your direction of travel).
2. Without moving the base, turn the integral compass capsule so that north ('N') lines up with the north-south grid lines on the map, adding or subtracting the declination.
3. Now take the compass off the map and simply follow the 'direction of travel' arrow on the compass by holding it out in front of you, sighting a landmark which is in the right direction, and walking towards it.
This exercise should be repeated, most often in bad weather, until you reach your destination.

Left: Electronic compasses such
as this one incorporate techno-
logy which was initially developed for military use.

Right: The Global Positioning
System (GPS) has revolutionised
navigation. Information calcu-
lated from satellite signals can
give the walker's position to
within 15 metres.

GPS AND ALTIMETERS

The GPS (Global Positioning System) has revolutionised navigation for walkers in the past
decade. Despite some initial scepticism and
high cost, it is now very widely used – for
example by the police and most British mountain rescue teams. And the cost of a GPS
receiver is now little more than that of a camera or a good quality waterproof jacket.

The Global Positioning System is operated
by the United States Department of Defense,
and was originally developed for military use by
the US Forces. It consists of 24 satellites orbit-
ing the earth every 12 hours on six different
planes at a common height of 19,500 kilometres (12,500 miles). These satellites transmit
positioning information computed from signals
picked up from ground-based stations all over
the world which are co-ordinated from the GPS
headquarters in Colorado Springs.

Signals from space

The accuracy of a GPS is
extremely impressive. It
works by locking on to the
signals from any four or
more of these satellites
simultaneously, and then
calculating your exact position and height above sea
level. In theory, and if
enough fixing satellites are
'visible' to the device, the
system can deliver your
position accurate to within
15 metres – not bad when
you consider that a normal
Ordnance Survey six-figure
grid reference is within
100 metres (109½ yards).

How to use GPS

Before you use your GPS,
you need to 'initialise' it –
that is, give it a first posi-
tional fix. You can speed this
up by telling the receiver
roughly where you are (if
you know!) by keying in
approximate co-ordinates or
by selecting the country
from a menu list. Once
you've done that once, and
providing you haven't moved
more than 482 kilometres
(300 miles) away from the
last time you switched on,
the machine only takes sec-
onds to give a reading.

Your GPS also needs to
be set to the appropriate
map which you are using –
for example, the Ordnance
Survey in Britain. GPS can
also be used to store posi-
tions in its memory as way-
markers – these can then
be linked together to form a
route and the receiver set to
navigate you along it. It can
also tell you your speed, the
estimated time of arrival and
the current time.

But GPS cannot tell you
how to read a map or give
you the kind of information
which is only available on a

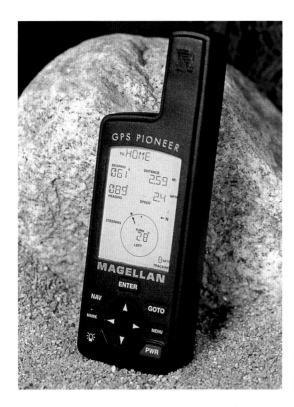

map. You will still need to understand the basic principles of navigation and compass bearings before you use one.

Altimeters

An instrument which will specifically tell you your height above sea level is the altimeter. These work by detecting differences in barometric pressure caused by climbing or descending and displaying this information as an accurate height above sea level.

They come in varying degrees of sophistication, from simple wrist-watch types, to the aneroid altimeter, which shows you your altitude by converting from the local air pressure.

Hand-held electronic altimeters are virtually mobile weather stations, showing barometric pressure, weather and pressure trends, and even giving a warning of forthcoming severe weather conditions.

Before using an altimeter, you need to set it at a known height, taken from a map. On calm days when the pressure is relatively stable, you will only need to correct your altimeter to a known height once or twice a day. But in unstable, stormy conditions, you might need to adjust it more often to give accurate readings.

As evening falls in the hills, it is especially important to keep a track of your exact position, in case you are benighted.

SLEEPING OUT

So you're now kitted out with all the gear, and you know where you're going and how to get there. The tempting prospect of that first camping trip beckons. Robert Louis Stevenson wrote: 'Night is a dead monotonous period under a roof; but in the open world it passes lightly...'. But which tent is best, and what about sleeping bags, camp food and hygiene?

TENTS: RIDGE AND GEODESIC

Choosing the right kind of tent for your personal requirements is a vital part of the preparation for a camping trip. Among the things you have to decide are how many people need to be accommodated, and whether you need to be near facilities, found only on recognised camp sites (a good idea on a first time trip), or whether are you going to 'rough it' with some wilderness camping out in the country.

Pitching your tent

Wherever you end up, some general rules about pitching your tent apply. You should choose a site which is reasonably flat and is free from stones. Avoid any site in a hollow as it will become colder at night and may be prone to flooding. Never, under any circumstances, pitch your tent on low-lying ground by a swollen river. Your tent door should face away from the prevailing wind if possible.

Usually the tent inner is erected first, attaching the poles and stretching the flysheet over the top, fixing it to the ground by guy ropes and pegs in the case of ridge or A-frame tents. With some tents, however, the flysheet is pitched first and then the inner is attached to the inside. All good quality tents should come with

pitching instructions.

The colour of your tent flysheet is a matter of personal choice, but most modern tents are produced in fairly subdued blues and greens so that they blend into the surrounding countryside and do not create too much 'visual pollution'.

Traditional A-frames

The most traditional type of tent is the ridge or 'A-frame' tent, much loved by Boy Scouts and Girl Guides, and the type of tent in which many people had their first camping experience.

If it is pitched properly on level ground, it is a reasonably stable structure. But A-frame tents are not free-standing, needing large diameter tent poles and long guy-ropes. Also, the sharp corners created by the A-frame mean that these tents are not the most efficient in their use of space.

The traditional 'A-frame' tent is still favoured by many campers, although increasing numbers now plump for geodesic dome tents.

From erecting a tent (far left) to camp cooking (left), camp skills are made easier by geodesic tents that are simple and practical.

Modern A-frame tents have sewn-in waterproof nylon groundsheets and separate breathable flysheets, which minimise condensation and can be extended over the entrance to give more space for cooking and the storage of equipment.

Modern geodesics

Many modern campers, and even mountaineers on expeditions, prefer geodesic tents. Geodesic tents – the name literally means curved like the earth's surface – are much more space-efficient and stable than A-frame tents. Their flexible poles stretch all over the surface of the tent, creating a self-supporting and very solid structure. Some geodesic tents are fitted with covered porches around the door, which are useful for cooking in wet or windy weather. Again, their groundsheets are usually made from waterproof nylon and the flysheet from coated polyester. The inners are made from breathable nylon or polyester and the tent poles are usually made from fibreglass.

Ten tips for campers

1. Look for a sheltered site
2. Try to find a flat spot, free from stones
3. Don't camp in a hollow, or too close to a swollen river
4. Face your tent door away from the prevailing wind
5. Erect the tent inner or flysheet first
6. Leave wet clothes to dry out in the tent porch
7. Don't cook inside the tent
8. Organise the inside of the tent so you can exit quickly in an emergency
9. Site your 'toilet' at least 100 metres (109 yards) from water
10. Leave the camp site as you found it

The modern geodesic tent is very efficient on space and easy to erect, and has the advantage of being self-supporting and stable in windy conditions.

TENTS: FAMILY, DOME AND TUNNEL

If there's one thing that most young children enjoy, it's the adventure of camping out in the countryside. It's the one occasion when there's no problem about getting them to go to bed, because the idea of sleeping out under canvas is perhaps the most exciting part of the whole experience for them. And once the initial excitement has worn off and they've settled down, the fresh air will ensure a sound sleep and a quiet night for all.

Holiday homes

To get the most from your camping holiday it is essential to select the right equipment, and your tent is unquestionably your most important piece of equipment. The size of the tent you choose will obviously depend on the size of your family. Some families prefer to all sleep in the same tent, while others put the children in one and the parents in another.

Family tents

At one extreme is the full-sized trailer-tent, carried in a trailer behind the car and erected into a mini-house

A large geodesic, family-sized tent, complete with canopy-type porch and room dividers, suitable for the larger family.

on the camp site. This is probably most suitable for a very young family – or for parents not prepared to totally 'rough it'. Many of these giant tents have windows, and properly divided rooms, separating the sleeping from the living and cooking facilities. Spacious canopies are also provided which are suitable for outdoor barbecues and similar activities.

    The larger A-frame and ridge tents are big enough to sleep up to ten people,

A dome tent in use on a mountaineering expedition, the purpose for which they were originally developed.

The dome tent was evolved to give more internal, usable space within the tent than is possible with the traditional ridge design. Built around three flexible poles which meet at the top of the tent, it provides a free-standing structure with more headroom than ridge, A-frame or tunnel tents. In times of high wind, however, this height off the ground can become something of a disadvantage.

Tunnel tents

The simplest type of tent is the tunnel or single-hoop, one-person tent. The construction of the tunnel tent consists of two or more hoops running across the width of the tent, creating the tunnel effect. The steeply-sloping sides of these tents and the fact that the hoops are not linked means that they can be subject to bending during high winds.

The single hoop or one-man tent design is the lightest tent of all, with an excellent space-to-weight ratio, making it perfect for lightweight backpacking or solo mountain expeditions. These tents are also popular with cycle tourists. If they are pitched correctly, with the hoop parallel to the prevailing wind, these light, low tents are surprisingly wind-resistant.

and have features such as sewn-in groundsheets, large storage pockets around the sides and 'walls' to keep out mud.

Domes tents

On a much smaller, and usually lighter, scale are the dome and tunnel tents, which can also be for family use but are more usually the preserve of individuals for 'wilderness' camping, away from the facilities provided by an official camp site.

A simple one- or two-person tunnel tent, consisting of two hoops across the tent which can be prone to bending in the wind.

SLEEPING BAGS

Getting a good night's sleep is very important, especially after a day's walking when you've been pushing your body much harder than usual. So once you have set up your tent, you'll need a good sleeping bag to curl up in for that well-earned rest.

Before buying a sleeping bag, you need to ask yourself when and how you will be using it. It may be that you want a sleeping bag which is suitable for regular camping trips, or you may want to carry one as part of your backpacking equipment. Or it may be that you will mainly be using it as an extra 'bed' when you have visitors at home.

Choosing a bag

Sleeping bags are rated according to their seasonal use. A one-season bag, therefore, is designed for use only in summer; a two-season bag would be suitable for use from late spring to early autumn; and a three-season bag would be adequate for use from the end of winter to the end of autumn. The top-rated bags are four-season and suitable for use throughout the winter, but conversely would be much too warm for people only using them during the summertime.

These ratings are based on use in valleys, so if you are going to be camping higher in the hills, where conditions are colder, especially at night, you will need to make allowances for that.

Size and filling

Make sure you get the right length of sleeping bag. Big is not necessarily best. If you are fairly short, it's no good getting an extra long bag because it will not be as efficient or warm as one which fits you snugly. Many manufacturers now offer different lengths of bags. Look out for a good hood and shoulder and neck collar to cover the head in really cold conditions, and a strong and serviceable two-way zip which can be useful in providing ventilation when you get really warm.

Sleeping bags come with either natural down or synthetic fillings. Down (or

Left: A synthetic-filled sleeping bag, with drawcords at the top and a generous hood and space for the feet.

Left, above: Sleeping bags compressed and packed into their bags ready for carrying in the rucksack.

The anatomy of a sleeping bag, showing hood, neck baffle, anti-snag zip with baffle, and 'circle' foot space for extra warmth.

feathers) traps heat very effectively and is quite light but bulky. For a sleeping bag to be called a down bag, it must have a minimum of 85 per cent down in its filling. Synthetically-filled sleeping bags consist of filaments of polyester fibre which trap heat between them.

Camping mats

As you will be sleeping on the ground, it's always a good idea to have a layer of insulation between your body and the groundsheet in the form of a camping mat. You will lose a lot of heat if you just rely on the groundsheet and a sleeping bag. Mats can be of either open- or closed-cell foam, the closed-cell variety, such as the Karrimat, is the most popular. These are resistant to compression and can absorb small amounts of water but cannot be reduced in size for packing.

The open-cell foam variety is lighter and needs an airtight cover, and tends to provide better insulation and be more comfortable than the closed-cell versions. Conventional airbeds are impractical for lightweight camping, but can be used in trailer-tents.

Keep it dry

A good sleeping bag will come with a cover, but even this may not be enough to keep it dry in a full-on downpour. If your sleeping bag is exposed and you think a storm is brewing, cover it in a polythene bag.

A pair of camping mats, essential for a comfortable night if you are camping out on the ground in the wilds.

A double-hooped bivouac bag (top) gives you that little bit more space than the traditional bivvy bag. This example of the traditional bag (left) has a handy diagonal zip, allowing easier access to the bag, which is a useful advantage if you are camping fully-clothed.

BIVVY BAGS AND TARPS

If you really want to enjoy Robert Louis Stevenson's 'Night among the Pines' quoted in the introduction to this section, then like him you will eventually be tempted to sleep out under the stars. This is the ultimate wilderness experience, where your only ceiling is the sky, your walls perhaps a silhouetted ring of trees or distant mountain peaks, and your morning alarm call the first warming rays of sunlight shafting through the branches.

Under the stars

Of course, you will need to be thoroughly experienced in the ways of the outdoors before this type of overnight stay can be recommended. But there is nothing quite like your first night truly out in the open to make you feel as though you have become an integral part of the landscape through which you have been walking.

Much will, of course, depend on the weather if you are really going to enjoy the true 'back to nature' experience which is provided by a bivouac. The other vitally-important factor will be having the right kind of equipment to cope with a night in the open air. And that usually means a bivouac or 'bivvy' bag, a bivvy tent or a tarpaulin (usually shortened to a 'tarp').

The advantage of all three options over a tent, is that they are much lighter and easier to carry, and there's no messing around like there is in pitching a tent. You just set down

wherever you feel like it, and, because all three alternatives are eminently adaptable to ground conditions, they can often be used where it would be impossible to pitch a tent.

Bivvy bags

Bivvy bags are basically waterproof sleeping bag covers with a bit of space to stow your clothes and other equipment. They should be made of breathable as well as waterproof material, or else condensation can become a problem. They should have a good hood, to keep out the rain and insects, and a good draw-

cord enclosure. Survival bags, usually made of polythene, should only be used in emergency situations.

Bivvy tents

Bivvy tents are really a cross between a small, lightweight tunnel tent and a bivvy bag. The addition of hooped

A bivouac bag can be made even more snug and secure in snowy conditions if it is secured by banks of snow. This example is in use on a cross-country ski-mountaineering trip.

supports gives you a significant amount of space inside than a traditional bivvy bag, although there's rarely enough space to allow you to sit up. They are much more comfortable than a bivvy bag during prolonged periods of wet weather camping.

Tarps

Outdoor 'tarps', or tarpaulins, are nothing like the heavy-duty rubberised or plastic sheets used by the Forces or workmen covering a hole dug in the street. They are usually made from water-proofed nylon and used in combination with a bivvy bag

or tent to provide you with more dry space in which to live or cook in the outdoors.

They are a very versatile piece of equipment, once you've got the hang of pitching them using available means of support, such as branches or even your own trekking poles.

STOVES

Sooner or later – and it is more likely to be sooner – all this fresh air will start to make you feel very hungry. So not long after you've pitched camp, you'll start to think about getting something hot to eat.

There are two main types of camping stoves – those which are fuelled by pressurised gas containers and those which use liquid fuel, which requires pressure and priming to ignite.

It is very important to decide which type of fuel you prefer when choosing your stove, because not all fuels are available in all countries, and the type of fuel you use is crucial to your stove's performance. Generally speaking, gas fuel is more expensive but cleaner, and liquid fuel is messier but cheaper.

Gas stoves

Cannisters of bottled gas, most usually butane, come as either self-sealing or non-sealing. Self sealing cannisters can be unscrewed from the stove when partially used. The non-sealing type require greater care and space when being transported, as they must remain attached to the stove at all times.

Although the use and availability of these butane gas canisters is spreading, they are not always available, especially in developing countries. They are freely available, however, in Britain, Europe and the

This multi-fuel stove can use petrol or kerosene. It is a cheaper, although messier alternative to a gas stove.

If you are camping with a larger group or family, then a camping grill, like this, is a useful addition to your equipment.

United States.

Gas stoves work efficiently in almost every environment, they are cheap, clean and easy to light as they fire up instantly. The drawbacks are that the fuel is relatively expensive and the heat output declines as the canister empties.

Liquid fuels

Petrol or kerosene stoves have the disadvantages that they have to be preheated, or primed, before use and can be messy and fiddly to light and keep clean. They are also much smellier than gas stoves. However, they produce a strong flame and

A small gas camping stove. Durable, small and easy to use – ideal for one or two walkers.

can burn for a long time on a single tank of fuel, which is much cheaper than the gas alternative. It is important to note that petrol and kerosene stoves produce a large, highly volatile flame in the priming stage, which

Walking in the outdoors gives you a healthy appetite, so getting the stove on is essential after you've pitched your tent.

should not be executed in the tent or its porch or near flammable fabric.

Multi-fuel and meths stoves

Multi-fuel stoves can, as the name suggests, use more

than one type of liquid fuel, but require a jet or fuel line to be swapped over whenever the fuel is changed.

Finally there are the stoves, such as Trangias, which use methylated spirits. This odour-free fuel evapo-

rates quickly when spilled, but its heat output is low and it is quite expensive. One advantage is that these stoves are very compact and often come with pans, burner and windshield all in the same stable cooking unit. Meths stoves are popular with youth groups such as the Scouts because they burn a non-pressurised fuel in a simple burner unit, making them probably the safest and easiest stoves to use.

FOOD AND DRINK

It's been estimated that the energy requirements of a normal day's walking – say 15–20
kilometres (9–12 miles) over six or seven
hours – are equivalent to those needed for a
day's housework or light manual work such
as painting.

So your dietary requirements for walking
are neither more nor less than for your normal
life, but you should avoid too much saturated
fat such as fatty meat and dairy products, and
sugary foods such as sugar and chocolate.

Eat to walk

In these diet-conscious
days, there are specialist
walking diets, usually linked
with a defined walking exercise programme (see Fit-
ness walking, page 22).
Carbohydrate is the fuel on
which your body runs. It's
stored in the liver and muscles as glycogen. Good
sources of carbohydrate
include potatoes, pasta, rice
and bread.

On a day-long walk it is
important to take enough
food along, because you will
be burning up energy which
needs to be replaced. It is
as well to take more food
than you think you'll need,
rather than less. Pack your
food carefully in the rucksack – there's nothing more
unappetising than a com-
pressed sandwich which
has been crushed at the
bottom of your pack for half
a day. Use lightweight polythene boxes if possible.

Fill your tanks

Small, sweet apples,
bananas, or nuts and raisins
can provide instant energy.
Energy bars and drinks con-

**Above: A young camper tucks in
to a camp-cooked meal with rel-
ish, having worked up a healthy
appetite on the trail all day.**

**Above, left: A wide range of
compact and surprisingly-tasty
dehydrated or freeze-dried foods
is available today.**

taining high levels of carbo-
hydrates are also a great way
to keep going on long, exerting walks. Outdoor and
cycling shops sell these specialist foods, but beware they
are expensive.

Dried food

If you are backpacking and
camping, you'll require
more calories than on day
walks. But as you are

carrying everything with you, you have the problem of keeping the weight down. Dried food is the answer. There is a wide range of lightweight dehydrated or freeze-dried foods available from outdoor shops – some of these are quite tasty and they have the advantage that they heat up quickly.

If you really want to go back to nature, then there's nothing better than having your meal by a roaring campfire – but make sure you keep it under control.

Drinks

Drink is very important, as you will lose a lot of fluid through perspiration, especially on a hot day when you are doing a lot of climbing.

But don't wait until you're feeling sluggish before taking a drink, as by then it's too late. Try to take on fluids regularly in small quantities. And after a summer walk, always drink plenty at the end of the day.

Watch out though, because not all drinks will help your rehydration. Alcoholic drinks, tea and coffee are all diuretic, so leave them alone and head for a cool fruit juice and water combination.

Stream water

Take care when drinking water direct from streams, especially in lowland areas. Untreated water can contain parasites, bacteria, viruses and chemicals, so it is best to either boil this water, treat it with chemical tablets such as chlorine or iodine, or use a filter.

CAMP HYGIENE

It was the US National Park Service that first came up with the maxim: 'Take only photographs, leave only footprints'. And that should be the aim of any walker visiting the countryside, whether it be a National Park, your local country park or anywhere else.

Another American slogan, aimed specifically at the backpacker or camper, is equally valid, and says: 'Pack it in, pack it out'. It simply means that anything you bring into the countryside should be taken out with you when you leave. While this obviously applies to unsightly detritus such as litter, it also reinforces the idea that you should try to leave no trace of your passing at all.

Personal hygiene

Campers and backpackers have a particular responsibility in this area, especially if they are 'wild' camping, away from recognised official campsites. This particularly applies to watercourses – all wild country 'toilets' should be at least 100 metres (109 yards) away from water supplies and the results should be buried 15-20 cm (6–8 inches) deep using a light metal or plastic trowel. Toilet paper can be burned if it is safe to do so, and you should wipe your hands with cleaning wipes.

Washing up

After you've set up camp and had your first meal, you are faced with the problem of washing up.

A camper washes in a mountain stream. This is usually fine if the stream is unpolluted and fast-flowing, but don't pollute it yourself with soap.

Although it seems like the easiest method, you should try to avoid washing your pots in the nearest lake or stream. Other people downstream from your camp site might drink the water polluted by your scraps of food. Scavenging animals such as rats and foxes might also be attracted by the remains of your meal.

Instead, you should use water from a container to wash up, scraping off the more stubborn bits of food with stones. Don't use washing-up liquid, as this could be a serious pollutant to natural water courses. And when you've finished, pour the dirty water directly into the ground, well away from lakes or streams.

'Pack it out'

Any scraps of food left should be taken away when you leave, as should pieces of litter such as empty packaging or used gas cartridges. As you leave your camp site, check that you haven't left anything behind and that it is clean and tidy. Ideally, there should be no sign of your stay at all.

Following these principles is known as 'no-trace camping', which suggests that previously unused sites should normally be avoided and, if used, never altered. Even in the wildest of wild country situations, the best camp sites will have been used before and should be re-used before a new site is set up. The rocks you use to hold down your tent pegs or to contain a camp fire should be returned to where you found them before you leave. Remember: 'Take only photographs, leave only footprints'.

Washing up is a chore which has to be done, even when you're camping. Make sure that you don't use washing-up liquid, however, as this can pollute.

TRAIL SKILLS

There are some things the walker can only learn from experience, and as your walking career extends you'll pick up certain pieces of knowledge which can best be described as 'trail skills'. These include anticipating a change in the weather, and knowing how to adapt your walking and equipment to various conditions.

READING
THE WEATHER

Samuel Johnson, the 18th century English lexicographer and critic, once wrote: 'When two Englishmen meet, their first talk is of the weather.' The same is still true today, and certainly the state of the weather is usually one of the first topics of conversation when walkers of any nationality meet on a path.

There's a very good reason for this. The weather can determine your enjoyment of the walk, how far you go, and in mountain or hill walking situations whether you should continue your walk at all or turn back.

Forecasts

Before commencing any walk it is essential to get a reliable, official weather forecast. These can be obtained from radio or television, and, in popular walking areas, from nearby information or visitor centres. There are also daily updated 'Weatherline' telephone numbers in most popular areas. The Internet is another useful source of weather reports, particularly if you are travelling abroad. Bear in mind that in hilly or mountainous areas the weather is notoriously fickle, and conditions can change within a matter of minutes.

Altitude plays a big part in weather changes – the temperature usually falls as you climb at a rate of about

You need to be aware of the dangers of walking in low cloud or mist when walking in the hills with precipices like this.

Reading the signs of changes in the weather is particularly important when walking in the hills, when mist can close in suddenly and without warning.

six degrees Celsius for every 100 metres climbed (or three degrees Fahrenheit for every 1,000 feet). Mist and low cloud are also much more frequent in the hills, leading to navigational problems and chilling. Thunderstorms, with the possibility of lightning strikes, are another hazard in the hills. If you are caught out in a thunderstorm, it is a good idea to drop down from high ridges and summits and keep well away from prominent objects such as rock pinnacles and metal structures or objects like ice axes which could attract lightning.

Wind-chill is another factor which must be considered when walking in the

hills. This is the amount of extra chilling or temperature drop perceived by the walker in high winds. Almost invariably, winds are much stronger at altitude than they are in the lowlands, so layering with warm, wind-proof clothing is essential (see Upland walking page 16 and Chapter 4 on clothing).

Weather proverbs

It is useful to be able to anticipate changes in the weather before they actually occur, and some of the traditional weather proverbs can usually be trusted, such as 'Red sky at night, shepherd's delight', and its opposite, 'Red sky in the morning, shepherd's warn-ing'. Another saying, 'Rain before seven, fine by eleven', has often been proved correct in the British climate. Other sayings such as that if cows are sitting down, it is bound to rain, are a little less reliable!

Finally, if you are experienced, properly equipped and not going too high into

Lowering cloud like this at the end of a day on a coastal path can presage the coming of rain in the near future.

the mountains, you can usually enjoy your walk, whatever the weather. As the 19th century English author, art critic and conservationist John Ruskin said:

'There is really no such thing as bad weather, only different kinds of good weather'.

WINTER WALKING

Many walkers put away their boots and rucksacks as soon as the leaves start to fall and the temperatures drop at the approach of winter. But they are missing out on some of the most wonderful experiences available in the great outdoors, because winter walking can provide the well-equipped walker with some truly memorable days.

Winter wonderland

The tourists who swarm to the 'honeypots' in summer all seem to be hibernating like bears and some other mammals. The countryside is swept bare of the billowing foliage that cloaked it, leaving the skeletal shapes of trees and a clarity of air and views which is often unsurpassed. A fall of snow or a heavy frost can transform a familiar landscape into a fairyland of exquisite beauty.

But winter walking demands special skills and proper equipment if it is to be enjoyed to the full. This

These well wrapped-up walkers seem equipped for anything as they trek through a snowy landscape in Norway.

is when your clothing and equipment really come into their own, and the money spent on a good water- and wind-proof jacket, decent boots and warm wear will handsomely repay itself.

Keeping warm

The layering system, described in Chapter 4, is very important in winter walking. As you work harder by, for example, climbing a hill, you may want to discard some layers to feel more comfortable. But by the time you reach the top of the hill, the chances are that you'll want to put them on again to keep out the chill. That's when the convenience of carrying a good rucksack also comes in.

Probably the greatest danger to the walker in winter is hypothermia or exposure, which occurs when the body is chilled to such an extent that the core temperature falls. Initially this affects the extremeties, but the core temperature can fall so much that it cannot maintain vital organs. The risk of exposure is increased by the strength of the wind and also by fatigue and hunger. The symptoms are usually uncertainty, stumbling, confusion and a failing sense of reality. The antidote is to provide rest, warmth and food as quickly as possible.

Walking in snow

Remember that walking in newly-fallen snow is much harder than walking on a clear path, in terms of both the physical effort required and finding your way. So you must be prepared to put a little more energy into just walking and into navigation if you are to make the most of your winter walks. This will mean that you will be unable to cover the same distances that you can in summer, and you may want to don those gaiters to keep the snow out of your boots and socks. Walking in the mountains during winter is an altogether more serious

A party of walkers enjoy a day of good snow and sunshine as they trek on a high-level route through the Alps.

proposition, and should only be attempted by really experienced parties. Ice and snow in the hills can be extremely dangerous for the unprepared. In exposed situations, for example on a ridge, it may be necessary to use an ice axe. Some knowledge of avalanche conditions and how to avoid them is also essential if you plan to take up the challenge of a snowy hill walk.

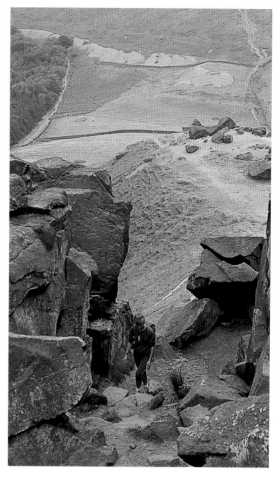

UPHILL AND DOWNHILL WALKING

Alfred Wainwright, doyen of English fell-walkers, believed that the only advice worth giving about walking – and he didn't even think this should be necessary – was to watch where you are putting your feet.

A controlled fall

In essence, of course, Wainwright was right. Walking is one of the first skills we learn at our mother's knee, and it is simply a matter of staying balanced on foot while moving forwards in what is technically a kind of continuous controlled fall. And when you are walking on rough paths or in the hills, you obviously have to take more care than when walking along a pavement in town. But there are a few useful tips about walking up and down hill which might be handy for people taking up walking as a hobby.

The first thing to say is that you should adopt a relaxed posture, with a straight back and arms swinging easily by your sides. Find a pace which is comfortable to you. Learn-

ing how to pace yourself is one of the secrets of good, strong walkers, who can keep going at apparently the same easy pace all day long. Actually, they will be constantly adapting their pace to the terrain over which they are passing.

Going up

So when walking uphill, for example, the stride pattern should be shortened – take shorter, less strenuous steps as you climb – and slow your pace to what is a comfortable level. You're bound to get out of breath when

Ascending a rocky gorge like this requires a little extra care about where you are putting your feet.

walking uphill for any length of time – and it's good for your metabolism if you do. It simply means that you are working your body harder and it is calling for more energy-giving oxygen. If you get too breathless, you may have to stop for a 'breather' – and you can always claim that you're just admiring the view! But more experienced walkers can usually keep going at their own steady pace, whatever the severity of the slope. When there are

no paths and you have to ascend or descend a steep slope, it's often a good idea to zig-zag up it (just as most well-used paths do). This eases the gradient into more manageable sections. It is always harder to attack a slope head-on.

Coming down

It is a statistical fact that most accidents to walkers happen when they are coming downhill. You are usually more relaxed, having done the hard, uphill work, and you have gravity on your side to help you descend.

Left: Crossing the top of a waterfall in the hills also requires a sure step and a steady head.

Below: When descending a scree slope like this, the walker should position his feet horizontal to the slope for maximum control.

That's the danger, of course, and gravity can work very seriously against you if you slip and fall.

So take extra care when you descend, adopting that Wainwright rule of watching where you put your feet. Try to keep them horizontal or even pointing slightly uphill, so that you can take advantage of any stones or ledges which will give you a better foothold. You are much more likely to slip if your feet are pointing downhill. Small, sideways steps are a much safer idea.

Think of others

And finally, if you are in the hills, try not to dislodge stones whether you are ascending or descending. You never know who is below you.

It's easy to lose your bearings when walking through a feature-less forest like this, especially when it is misty.

FOREST WALKING

There are few greater pleasures available to the walker than that of walking through the cool shade of a woodland on a hot, early summer's day. The leafy green canopy of the trees will be filled with birdsong, and the dappled shade it creates will provide a welcome relief from the intense heat of the sun.

Autumn is another wonderful time for woodland or forest walks, when the glorious colours of the changing leaves light up your way, and the only sound is the satisfying swish and crunch of your boots through the carpet of fallen leaves. In winter and spring, exciting glimpses of new views are revealed through the naked branches of the trees which, if they are covered in snow, create another wonderland.

Following the trail

Most forest trails are very easy to follow, because they have to use existing tracks or rides through the trees. This is especially true in planted forests, where the closely-packed trees, usually conifers, are almost impenetrable without a bull-dozer or a machete knife. On official long-distance routes such as the Appalachian Trail in the eastern USA and the Pennine Way through the conifers of the Border Forest, the path is also way-marked at junctions where

there is any doubt, so you can't go far wrong. Many forestry authorities, such as the Forestry Commission in Britain, are now keen to open up their forests for recreational use, and provide easy-to-follow self-guided trails through many of their properties. These often take the form of nature trails, with points of added interest to watch out for and picnic sites along the route.

If you do get lost in a forest the best thing to do is to follow one of the forest rides, all of which will eventually lead to a road or some form of habitation. You should look out for beaten tracks, boot prints or broken branches to regain your path. If you don't have a compass, north can usually be found by the fact that the moss growing on the trunks of trees normally grows on that side.

Wild camping and wildlife

If you are backpacking and camping in the woods, you must take extra care to

avoid starting fires, especially in the dry summer season. Use recognised camp sites where possible, but if you are 'wild' camping, ensure that you carefully extinguish any fires and leave your camp site as you found it. And you must hang your food supplies from a convenient branch overnight if you are camping in bear country, especially in the USA, as you don't want an uninvited guest dinner! The wildlife which you may well encounter on your woodland walks might include squirrels, foxes, badgers and many varieties of deer, in addition to a wide range of bird life including woodland specialists such as woodpeckers and owls. But you will have to try not to make too much noise kicking up the leaves, because woodland wildlife is invariably shy.

Above: The mother and toddler here are seen admiring the plant life on a sunlit woodland path.

Right: Woodlands can be magical places in the autumn, when the leaves start to change colour and sunlight dapples the path.

COASTAL WALKING

In the words of the old music hall song, most of us really do like to 'be beside the seaside'. And walking along the coast is a great way to appreciate the geology of the shoreline and the varied wildlife of this habitat.

There are many different kinds of coastal walking, from trudging through sandy dunes and crunching across pebble beaches – which can be just as exhausting a surface for walking on as mud or snow – to airy promenades along switchback cliffs, with the waves crashing far below your feet and seabirds soaring and screaming in the thermals above.

Shoreline stroll

Coastal walking can also take-in the simple, childish pleasures of beach-combing or investigating the pools of a rocky foreshore, all of which make the coast one of the most fascinating of places in which to walk. No special skills are required, and it's almost impossible to get lost on a coastal walk – you just keep the sea to one side! But you must keep an eye on the weather because, like in the mountains, it can change very quickly on the coast, and you must be prepared for it with adequate equipment and clothing. When walking along the coast, you can usually see any changes coming, especially if they are coming from the sea. Your equipment must match the coast's unpredictability and you should be ready for anything the weather can throw at you.

Potential dangers

Cliff-top walking is every bit as dangerous as hill walking, and you should take extra care about where you put your feet on narrow, cliff paths, which were often originally used by coastguards or fishermen. There can be a dangerous drop to one side in these situations, and you must not stray too close to the edge, especially in the frequently stormy conditions which are found on the coast. If you are

A lone walker strides out on the South West Coast Path, England. Undulating cliff paths are commonplace in coastal walking.

crossing a bay or to an island across sands which are subject to tide races, make sure that you know the times of the high tide before you set out. Many walkers have been marooned, have had to be rescued or have even drowned because they did not take this elementary precaution. Some tides can come in at the speed of a galloping horse, so you are unlikely to outrun them.

Walk with the birds

Many long-distance walks follow the coast, such as the South West Peninsula or Pembrokeshire Coast National Trails in England and the Dingle Way in Ireland. Coastlines are great places for the study of marine bird life, especially those species which breed on cliff faces, so a pair of binoculars is a very useful addition to your kit when on a coastal walk. Watching a soaring peregrine falcon or gannet from a sunlit cliff-top is one of the great pleasures of walking along the coast.

A walker stops to admire the tremendous coastal scenery as Atlantic breakers crash in on this headland in Argyll, Scotland.

ACTIVITY HIKING

Taking note of what you see along the way can add to your enjoyment of a walk. Indeed there are many hobbies, birdwatching and botany for example, which cannot be enjoyed without a fair amount of walking to get to what you want to see. In this section, we'll look at some of the activities which can give 'added value' to your country walking.

ROCKS AND PLANTS

All landscapes ultimately depend on, and are shaped by, their geology. It is the rocks beneath which give the countryside its form and which also give it its distinctive vegetation and, thereby, wildlife.

Understanding the geology of an area can add a great deal of interest to any walk – you will start to realise how everything in nature is interdependent and why the landscape takes its particular form. A range of hills, for example, might be the remains of a subtropical coral reef laid down 350 million years ago, and it may contain fossils of sea lilies and other forms of long extinct life. A darker rock which outcrops into a distinctive, upstanding hill may be the remains of a long-extinct volcano which at one time blanketed the landscape in lava and ash. And a low-lying river valley may be flat because it was the site of a glacial lake during the Ice Age, 10,000 years ago, when mammoths roamed its shores.

Know your rocks

All rocks fall into one of three categories. Igneous rocks are formed by volcanic action deep within the earth, examples include granite and basalt. Sedimentary rocks, which are usually laid down in regular beds under settled conditions either underwater or by the action of the wind, include limestone, sandstone or chalk.

Metamorphic rocks are igneous or sedimentary rocks which have been changed in character by heat, pressure or chemical action, for example gneiss, schist, marble or slate.

A good field guide will enable you to identify the different types of rock, and will help you to recognise the different kinds of fossils which may be exposed in rock formations. You should not, however, take rock or fossil samples from outcrops without getting permission first. Photographs are usually a much less destructive alternative.

Botanical interests

Each type of rock gives rise to a different type of flora. It's a good idea to take along a field guide to wildflowers on your walk in summer, so you can identify all the different types of flowers you might come across. A mineral-rich limestone or chalk landscape usually has a wealth of wild flowers with their associated insects and animals. This is where you will find plants like orchids and gentians, for

Coastal cliffs are a good place to see the stratification of rocks, as seen above this walker's head as she admires a flow of tufa rock.

Nature's garden in the Mount Rainier National Park in Washington, USA. Alpine meadows like this provide some of the finest displays of wildflowers.

example, in the French Alps and Pyrenees or in the limestone gorges of Corsica. Sandstone hills, on the other hand, have a much more limited range of plant life, and the vegetation can often revert to moorland in Europe, where bogs form in the build-up of decaying vege-tation which eventually becomes peat. Here, only tough moor-land plants such as heather or bilberry can thrive in the harsh conditions.

An igneous or metamor-phic landscape, such as the granites found in the Appalachians or Adiron-dacks of the Eastern USA, and beneath the towering spires of the Yosemite National Park in the Californian Rockies, is also less rich in plant life, although there are excep-tions where minerals enrich the surface soil.

At lower altitudes, chalk or limestone meadows which have not been 'improved' by agriculture are usually well-blessed with wildflowers, and there are often fine woodlands. Even in sandstone country, native woodlands and un-improved meadows support a great variety of wildflowers and wildlife, so keep your eyes peeled!

BIRDWATCHING

One of the easiest and most rewarding pastimes which the walker can adopt is bird-watching. And you don't need a great deal of extra equipment weighing you down to do it.

A good pair of binoculars and an identi-fication book are all you need to open up a whole new world of interest and excitement. Modern compact binoculars give excellent magnification relative to their size, and they are easily slipped into your jacket pocket or rucksack.

Look and listen

You don't have to be an obsessive 'twitcher', eager to 'tick off' rarities, to enjoy a wide variety of bird life on your walks. The mere fact of getting away from the road and into the countryside means that you are far more likely to see birds than when confined to a car. If you become really hooked on birdwatching, you'll soon realise that plain, dull-coloured clothing is less likely to disturb birds, and you will learn to walk with your senses tuned to pick up the slightest movement in order to sight as many birds as possible. And you will know where and when you are most likely to see certain types of birds, as you pass through and recognise their individual habitats.

Varied habitats

If you are walking through woodland in the spring or early summer, for example, you may well hear more birds than you see. But once you have learned the different types of songs, it will not be long before you can pick out the warblers from the finches and you'll soon be spotting them as they flit through the trees. Obvious sounds such as the hammering of a wood-pecker are easier to identify, and then there's the excite-ment of seeing a bird of prey, such as an owl, spar-

A hillwaker ticks off another interesting bird on a trip in the mountains. His dog, however, may have other ideas!

rowhawk, buzzard gliding through or above the canopy of trees. Out in the open fields, song birds such as the skylark will quickly identify themselves, while riverside or lakeside walks can be enlivened by the sight of dippers, kingfishers, herons, coots or ducks and geese. Waders will attract the attention in wetter, wilder areas, or on estuaries or the coast, where cliff-top walks will be accompanied by the shouts, screams and spectacular aerobatics of seabirds such as gulls, terns and guillemots.

In the hills, bird life is less abundant but just as exciting. The heather moorlands of Britain, for example, will reveal waders like the curlew and plovers and the cackling call of the red grouse. The dashing flight of quartering birds of prey such as the merlin or harrier will enliven many a moorland stroll. A word of warning, however – such rare birds of prey are strictly protected, and it is an offence to deliberately disturb them, especially at nesting time. So the rule is, spot them and walk on.

King of Birds

But perhaps the ultimate birdwatching experience is in the mountains, the last refuge of much of our most spectacular wildlife. Here you may be lucky enough to see, effortlessly riding on the thermals above the pinnacles, the 'king of the birds' – the mighty eagle. There is surely no better sight with which to remind yourself of Nature's beauty.

Above: The kingfisher (*Alcedo atthis*) can often add a touch of colour and drama to a riverside walk. It usually returns to the same branch after it has caught its prey.

Left: Inland water provides an abundance of birdlife, such as this Great Blue Heron (*Ardea herodias*) patrolling the river's edge.

LANDSCAPE HISTORY

Almost every landscape the walker passes through – except perhaps the highest mountain tops, the Polar wilderness, coastal cliffs or the desert – has been altered in some way by Man. Even some of the most apparently wild places, such as mountain passes, moorland and marshland, have usually been adapted and in some cases created by Man's action, either directly by physical intervention or by the livestock farmer's introduction of domestic grazing animals.

Learning from the land

The walker is in a unique position to be able to 'read' man-made landscapes. By passing through them on foot, he or she can note the subtle changes humans have made, from the bumps and hollows in a grassy meadow which might indicate a former settlement, to more obvious features such as ruins, field patterns and boundaries, or prehistoric earthworks and

Ancient sites are not the only points of interest, historical buildings give a glimpse of the locality's more recent past.

standing stones. The study of landscape history is a relatively new science, introduced in Britain by the late Professor W.G. Hoskins. His simple philosophy, in a country so overlaid with various periods of history as Britain, was 'Everything is older than you think'. This truism is demonstrated by the recent discoveries that the clearance of the virgin forests which followed the end of the last Ice Age was begun

almost immediately by the first settlers of the Stone Age, and not during the Middle Ages as was once thought.

Recognising the signs

Prehistoric field systems and settlements are constantly being revealed by aerial photography in all parts of the world, and while they may not be immediately visible to the walker, the eye can be trained to pick up the slight embankments and ditches which can reveal a prehistoric past. Elsewhere, prehistoric landscapes can be

traced, such as in the limestone caves of the Dordogne in south-west France and the ruins of cliff-dwellings in places like the Mesa Verde National Park in Colorado in the western USA. Other prehistoric monuments punctuate the landscape of the Boyne valley in Ireland, and in the impressive hillforts of the west of Ireland and the Aran Islands.

Early industrial sites such as former mills can be found in the New England states of the USA, where many former mill buildings have been converted to houses.

Guidebooks to historical sites

It should be stressed that it is only through thorough historical research that firm conclusions can be drawn, and usually not until archaeological excavations have been carried out. But there are many excellent guidebooks which can direct the walker to historical landscapes, and the sense of continuity with the ancient past which is obtained from walking through some of these landscapes is one of the greatest thrills for the walker.

As J.R.L. Anderson wrote in his classic account of a walk along the prehistoric Ridgeway of southern Britain (now a National Trail), *The Oldest Road*:

'You walk in the footsteps of three hundred generations, seeing the same rounded hills, the same sky, tripping, it may be, over the same stone that stubbed a human toe ten thousand years ago.'

Above: Hadrian's Wall is an obvious man-made feature which ultilises the natural escarpment of the Whin Sill in Northumberland, England.

Right: Castles, such as Donnottar in Scotland (right), are an obvious highlight in the historical landscape.

Mountainous areas, with their clear light and superb scenery, provide wonderful opportunities for the walking photographer.

PHOTOGRAPHY

The vast majority of walkers now carry a camera with them on their rambles. This is usually just to record the highlights of the walk which they can look at later with friends or family. Other walkers specialise in landscape photography, and pride themselves on the quality and composition of their photographs, making it the major reason for their excursions. Among the most famous of these were Ansel Adams in the western National Parks of America, and Walter Poucher in the hills of Britain.

The advent of the small, compact and relatively inexpensive 35 mm camera has made it easy for the amateur to take photographs while out walking. And it has to be said that this combination can often achieve very good, professional-standard results.

Taking better pictures

Composition is all-important in landscape photography, and even the most expensive equipment cannot compensate for a lack of experience and skill in that direction.

Foreground, for example, is vitally important and can detract from an otherwise striking photograph. The use of a dynamically-placed figure or object such as a person or a tree can also improve a landscape photograph and give overall scale to the image.

Sun and snow

Lighting is another vital factor in a good landscape photograph. Many of the top professionals often get up very early in the day for their outdoor photographic sessions, or else they will wait until the sun is waning to get the best and strongest lighting effects.

Although many walkers seem only to take their photographs in high summer in bright, cloudless conditions, the light at that time of the year can often be quite 'flat' and lacking in contrast. Better cloud effects and stronger, contrasting colours are more often found in the countryside in springtime and autumn.

Winter is another often sadly neglected season for landscape photography, but it can provide the walker/photographer with some of the best opportunities for capturing memorable images. A snowfall can turn a mediocre shot of a mundane landscape into a magical fairyland of scintillating icicles and whipped cream drifts.

Experimenting with lenses can produce some impressive results. Here a low-cost fish-eye converter has been used to transform a standard panorama of the Grand Canyon.

Equipment

If the hobby of landscape photography really takes over on your walking trips, you will probably feel the need to invest in more expensive equipment, such as a better camera and a tripod. Of course, you will have to carry all this with you on your walks, and tripods can be quite awkward, although most are lightweight with telescopic legs. Special camera bags are also available which strap on around your waist and give safe and easy access to your camera, film, lenses and filters. It's always a good idea to carry a few extra rolls of film with you in the rucksack or camera bag – that striking shot always seems to turn up just as you are about to run out of film! Of course, once you've taken all those wonderful shots, you can look forward to the pleasure of showing them to your friends or family.

Ten tips for good landscape photography

1. Take plenty of film
2. Always protect your camera
3. Remember, composition is all-important
4. Use figures where possible for scale
5. Don't forget to include an interesting foreground
6. Always try to get a 'different' angle
7. Try to avoid 'flat' lighting conditions
8. Don't just take your pictures in summer
9. Try some shots in winter
10. Don't let the photography spoil the walk!

PAINTING AND SKETCHING

Most of the great artists of the world have enjoyed walking and the outdoors. Among many examples, J.M.W. Turner, one of the greatest masters of watercolour and the so-called 'artist of light', sketched his landscapes in all weathers, capturing the subtle changes in light which can only be seen in the outdoors.

The East Anglian artist John Constable claimed that the scenes he knew so well around his home on the Essex-Suffolk border were what made him a painter, while the artists of the Pre-Raphaelite school took inspiration from country landscapes. So it is neither new nor unnatural for walkers to want to record the scenes they so enjoy on their strolls by sketching or painting them.

Don't attract attention

According to David Bellamy, the distinguished modern wilderness watercolourist, you should not start out with a large easel, board and box of paints which shout 'artist' to the world. If you do, you will rapidly be surrounded by hordes of people offering you all sorts of advice. You should begin simply with an A5 sketchpad and a few well-sharpened pencils. Some people are quite timid about taking even a sketchpad along on their walks because of the attention it attracts, so Bellamy suggests hiding the sketchpad in a magazine or sketching with your back to a wall, so that people can't peer over your shoulder. Another alternative is to wear a large, wide-brimmed hat, which apparently will soon isolate you from any onlookers.

Choosing your subject

You should start by looking for a subject with a definite focal point, such as a building, bridge, tree, waterfall or other physical feature and walk around for a few moments to find what you consider to be the best viewpoint of it. Start your drawing with the feature which attracted you, and work outwards from that, sketching lightly at first and then putting in the detail more strongly. You should make notes on your sketch of the main colours of the scene for when you come to make a painting out of your sketch, which may be at a much larger scale.

Sometimes, back-up photographs taken at the scene will also help. Only after you have gained expe-

Portable and spiral bound sketch pads of the type which can be carried easily and used in the field.

rience of sketching with pencil should you move on to charcoal, pens, water-soluble pencils or water-colour paints. Again, your painting will only be a 'working document' type of sketch rather than the finished painting, so avoid the temptation of working it up into a finished piece.

With this type of outdoor sketching, there is no need to slavishly record every nuance of colour you see. You should pare down the countless greens in a summer scene, for example, to three or four at the most. Take full advantage of the changing light, just like Turner did, and to add interest include figures, which can be sketched in at the side of the sheet and added to the painting at a later date.

Water-colourist David Bellamy pauses on his walk to sketch a scene among the High Atlas Mountains of Morocco.

SCRAMBLING AND ORIENTEERING

This section looks at two extensions of walking – scrambling and orienteering – which the experienced walker may well progress towards. Scrambling is a difficult term to define, as it comes somewhere between walking and rock climbing in the overall scale of mountaineering skills.

A young couple enjoy a scramble up an easy crag in the mountains. Scrambling starts where walking ends.

Scrambling

Essentially, scrambling involves the use of hands as well as feet in ascending or descending situations in the hills, but it usually does not involve the use of ropes, as pure climbing does. Scrambling should only be attempted by experienced and competent hill walkers, and those who have a good head for heights. It is definitely a hobby to avoid if you are frightened by a certain amount of exposure on steep rock.

It follows that scrambling is a special skill which should not be attempted by beginners in the walking game. One of the best definitions of scrambling is that it begins where walking ends, and ends where rock climbing begins.

Using your head

As well as involving the use of your hands, scrambling also brings another important part of the body into play: your head. In scrambling up or down a steep place, it is vital that you think ahead as to where your actions will take you, which is the best route (or 'line') or how you will overcome the next awkward step. There will be times when the use of a rope is advisable, because an unroped scrambler is virtually soloing a climb in which the consequences of a fall could be extremely serious. In these situations, you will need some knowledge of the belaying techniques of the rock climber. Unroped scrambling in exposed situations is actually much more dangerous than roped, and therefore protected, climbing.

It should be mentioned that hill walkers, especially on ridge walks, will often find themselves having to do a little bit of scrambling, using their hands for additional support. Examples of this include: the Aonach Eagach ride in Glencoe, Scotland; the Via delle Bocchette in the Italian Dolomites; and the Corsican High Level Route on that lovely Mediterranean island.

Above: Scrambling on jagged outcrops may require a rope. This is where scrambling verges on mountaineering.

Right: Orienteers approach a marker in open country through young bracken on an orienteering course in the mountains.

But having dispensed the obligatory 'health warnings', for the experienced hill walker, scrambling can be one of the purest and most enjoyable branches of the sport, giving a real sense of freedom and achievement.

Cunning running

The head also has to be used in orienteering, once described as 'the art of cunning running'. Originating in Scandinavia, this sport involves finding your way with the aid of map and compass between a series of control points, usually in wild country or forests, as quickly as possible. Courses of different lengths and difficulty are usually available at orienteering events, and all can be walked in a non-competitive way, if preferred. Orienteering is an excellent way to hone your navigational skills. For this reason, many youth groups, including the Scouts, hold regular orienteering events for their members.

EMERGENCIES

The chances of having an accident while out walking are extremely remote. Walking is one of the safest and most healthy hobbies you can have, because it does not involve dangerous equipment which can fail, or any kind of physical contact. But, as with anything else, you should always be prepared for emergencies.

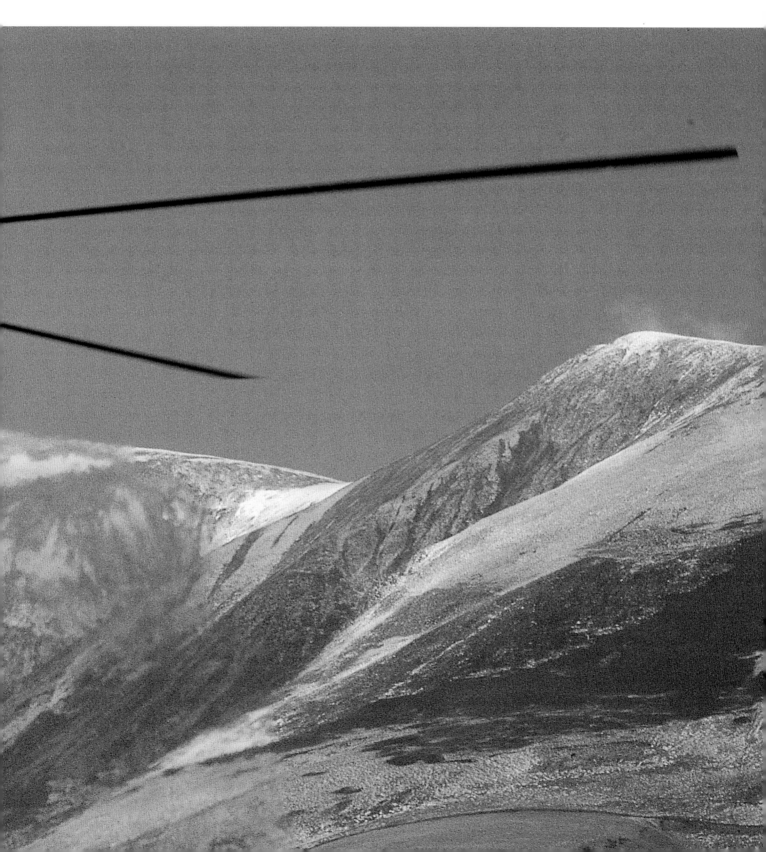

WHAT TO DO

Most experienced ramblers will tell you that accidents and emergencies are rare occurrences on country walks. However you should still be prepared, and by remembering a few simple tips you can prevent a situation deteriorating from accident to emergency. The most common accident while out walking is a fall, which might result in a sprained ankle or, at worst, a broken bone.

Stay calm

In the hills or remote countryside, an accident is likely to be much more serious because you will probably be a long way from any sort of assistance. In any kind of emergency the first imperative is to keep calm, find a sheltered spot and keep the injured person warm and comfortable. Administer whatever first aid you can (see Page 118), and decide what you have to do to evacuate the injured person. If you are in a situation where you cannot move because you are lost or

It is important to help one another in an emergency. Here, a couple of walkers assist a friend with an injured knee to safety.

weather conditions are really bad, you should use the International Distress Signal of six successive short blasts on your whistle, then wait for one minute before trying again. If you have a torch, you should give six short flashes at one minutes intervals.

Going for help

If it is possible for one of your party to go for help, make a careful note of

cramp, cuts or bruises, or bites from a dog or insects. All of these can be easily self-treated by simple first aid procedures, which are described in the following section on page 118.

Late but safe

If you arrive safely, but much later than you had originally intended back at your destination, you should make sure you contact the police to let them know you are safe. This will avoid a fruitless full-scale search being initiated.

Once help has arrived, here in the form of a rescue team, you should leave treatment and evacuation of the injured person to the professionals.

exactly where you are, with a grid reference if possible, and what the injury apparently is, so that the messenger can tell the emergency services all they need to know. This usually involves someone reaching the nearest telephone, dialling emergency services and asking for an ambulance. You should never rely on a mobile phone to get you out of trouble as very often the case that they do not work in the hills.

It is important that those left with the casualty should stay exactly where they are while the messengers go for help. Messengers should be prepared to return with the rescuers to lead them to the injured person. These points should only be used when you are dealing with a casualty who cannot be moved safely. However, the majority of walking accidents will not be as serious as this. Common minor mishaps might include blisters,

Ten tips in an emergency

1. **Keep calm**
2. **Find a sheltered spot and keep the casualty warm**
3. **Give whatever first aid you can**
4. **If the casualty cannot be moved, plan your next course of action**
5. **Make a note of your position**
6. **Send someone for help, usually to the nearest telephone**
7. **Don't rely on a mobile phone**
8. **If you cannot move, use the International Distress Signal**
   (six short blasts on a whistle or six flashes on a torch at one-minute intervals)
9. **If you've sent for help, stay where you are**
10. **If you arrive back late, tell the police**

FIRST AID

As already stated, most of the accidents which can befall the walker are likely to be of a minor nature, and usually can be self-treated by simple first aid procedures.

It is always advisable to carry a small first aid kit with you in your rucksack or jacket pocket. This should include items such as plasters for minor cuts, grazes or blisters; sterile wound dressings which will staunch bleeding; a crepe bandage to support sprained limbs; aspirin or paracetamol for pain relief; antiseptic cream to keep wounds clean; an insect repellent; scissors and safety pins. These first aid kits can be quite easily and cheaply made up yourself, or you can buy compact, ready-made kits especially designed for use in the outdoors.

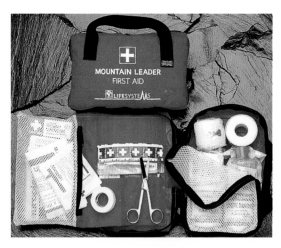

Carrying a first aid kit like this in your rucksack is always a good idea, especially on more strenuous or serious walking trips.

Hypothermia

In cases of hypothermia, or exposure, your plastic survival or bivvy bag (see page 80) should be used. The first signs of hypothermia are the onset of stumbling, confusion and uncertainty in the sufferer, and the first-aid treatment is to make the casualty as warm and dry as possible.

Cuts, bites and stings

Wounds such as cuts or scratches should be treated by first stopping the bleeding by applying a dressing, cleaning the wound with antiseptic cream or water, and then applying a sterile dressing or plaster depending on the size of the wound. Bites and stings are best treated by applying antiseptic cream.

Sprains and fractures

Stretching injuries such as sprains or strains are common among walkers, and they should be treated by stopping immediately and resting the affected limb. To stop swelling, you should apply cold water to the area

and elevate the limb. You should also wrap a cold, wet bandage firmly around the affected area in a figure of eight style, especially if it is an ankle which has been sprained – this may have to be placed over the boot, if the swelling has made it impossible to remove.

Fractures or broken bones are a common result of a fall. The symptoms are severe pain, swelling and bruising, with the broken bone sometimes protruding through the skin. The best treatment is to get to a hospital as soon as you can. First aid for a broken arm or collar bone, both common walking-fall injuries, is to rest and support the arm with a sling. You should support a broken leg by tying it to the patient's body or to a make-shift splint, such as trekking pole or stick, but you should not try to straighten any bent or deformed limbs.

Sunstroke

Sunstroke or sunburn is another common emergency for walkers. Sunburn can be treated by calamine lotion, but the best cure is

prevention via a high-factor sunscreen or wide-brimmed hat which also protects the neck. Sun or heat stroke is a life-threatening condition and an ambulance needs to be called for. Sufferers need to be put in the shade, covered with wet towels or bandages, or even have cold water poured over them. They should also be encouraged to drink as much as possible.

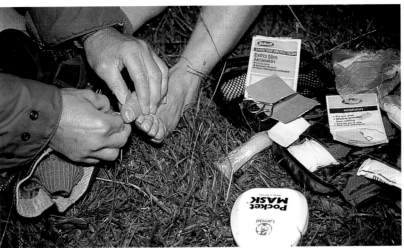

Above: Applying dressings and bandages is a skill in itself. The regular hill-walker should consider taking a first aid course.

Left: Blisters are the most common form of injury among walkers. Here a plaster from the first aid kit is applied to a blistered toe.

'GREEN' HIKING – SUSTAINABILITY

If you asked any walker about the need to conserve the countryside, it would be pretty safe to assume that they would say it was essential. All walkers enjoy the countryside and would not knowingly want to do anything to destroy it. Yet the sheer numbers of walkers in the most popular walking areas such as the National Parks are doing just that.

Erosion and restoration

Footpath and trail erosion has become a major problem in many areas of outstanding natural beauty and some paths have had to be diverted or even closed so that they can be restored and recover from the pounding effect of thousands of pairs of walkers' boots. Full-time teams of footpath restorers are now employed on all the National Trails, such as the

Far left: Responsible walkers will use public transport wherever possible.

Left: With a little planning and studying of timetables, you can work out linear walking routes which can return you to your starting point by bus or train.

Pennine Way in Britain. Paths are now 'floated' across peat bogs on geotextile mats, and paving slabs are air-lifted in to repair the damage done by overuse. Footpath restoration is now a major and ever-increasing part of every National Park service budget.

What is the answer?

After all, those walkers are just out enjoying the countryside. They are, to quote the US National Parks Service again, doing nothing more than 'taking only photographs and leaving only footprints'.

There are several things the walker can do to create a more sustainable countryside. First, you should try to avoid the most-used paths wherever you can, and especially in the busiest walking season, usually the summer. There are always plenty of less-crowded alternatives. Britain, for example, has over 225,000 kilometres (140,000) miles of rights of way, and these can take the walker into some beautiful, unspoiled and uncrowded countryside. There are also many miles of concessionary paths on water company and Forestry Commission land which are open to walkers.

Another way in which walkers can help to save the environment is to use public transport to get to and from their walks, and not always use their cars. In many places, public transport can be used to do linear walks, getting back to your starting point by bus or train, instead of the usual circular routes – compulsory for those using their own transport. It also cuts down on traffic congestion and pollution.

Most visitors to the National Parks are day visitors – that is they come and go home in a day, often spending nothing while they are there. A more sustainable alternative is to stay in local accommodation or to camp, using and supporting local shops and facilities and helping to ensure the continuation of a living landscape.

Some National Parks have set up a network of 'camping barns' which offer cheap and simple accommodation for walkers who don't want to carry tents. These buildings are often redundant to the farmer, and this new use restores them as traditional features in the landscape and also provides the farmer with a modest alternative source of income. 'Green' walkers will want to stick to paths and follow signposted diversions in order not to spread erosion any further than it has gone already. And they will take their litter home with them, along with those priceless photographs and memories.

HIKERS' CHECKLISTS

SUMMER WALKING
(The following list is appropriate for a simple, lowland day walk)

- Boots
- Shirt
- Lightweight fleece jacket or sweater
- Waterproof jacket
- Gaiters or waterproof trousers
- Hat, to give protection from the sun as well as the rain
- Trekking poles
- Rucksack (20-50 litres)
- Sit mat
- Lunch and drinks, cold and hot
- High-energy snacks
- Map
- Compass and/or GPS receiver
- Guidebook
- First aid kit, including sunscreen
- Emergency whistle
- Camera

WINTER WALKING

(The following list is appropriate for a simple lowland day walk)

- Boots
- Shirt
- Heavyweight fleece jacket or sweater
- Extra sweater
- Water- and wind-proof jacket
- Gaiters or waterproof trousers
- Warm hat or Balaclava, to give ear protection from the wind and rain
- Gloves
- Sunglasses, to stop snow glare
- Rucksack (30-60 litres)
- Trekking poles
- Sit mat
- Bivvy or survival bag
- Lunch and hot drink (Thermos)
- High-energy snacks
- Map
- Compass and/or GPS receiver
- Guidebook
- First aid kit, including sunscreen
- Emergency whistle
- Head lamp or torch, with spare batteries
- Camera

FAMILY WALKING

(The following list is appropriate for a simple lowland summer day walk with, say, two children)

- Boots
- Shirts
- Fleece jackets or sweaters
- Waterproof jackets
- Gaiters or waterproof trousers
- Hats, to give protection from the sun as well as the rain
- Rucksack (30-60 litres)
- Papoose(s)
- Sit mats
- Lunch and drinks, cold and hot
- Plenty of high-energy snacks
- Map
- Compass and/or GPS receiver
- Guidebook and wildlife identification guide
- First aid kit, including sunscreen
- Emergency whistle
- Camera

USEFUL ADDRESSES AND FURTHER READING

**Osterreichischer Alpenverein
(OAV)**
Wilhelm Greil Strasse 15
A-6010 Innsbruck
Austria

Grote Routepaden
Van Stralenstraat 40
B-2060 Antwerp
Belgium

**Les Sentiers de Grande Ran-
donee (SGR)**
Boite Postale 10
B-4000 Leige 1
Belgium

**Canadian
Volkssport Federation**
PO Box 2668
Station D
Ottawa
ON KIP 5W7
Canada

**Landsforeningen
Dansk Vandrelaug**
Kulturvet 7
DK-1175
Copenhagen K
Denmark

**Centre d'Information
de la FFRP**
14 rue Riquet
F-75019
Paris
France

**European Ramblers' Associa-
tion**
Wilhelmshoher Allee 157-159
D-34121
Kassel
Germany

**Verband Deutscher Gebirgs
und Wandervereine**
Wilhelmshoher Allee 157-159
D-34121
Kassel
Germany

Backpackers' Club
49 Lyndhurst Road
Exmouth
Devon
EX8 3DS
Great Britain

**Long Distance Walkers' Asso-
ciation**
21 Upcroft
Windsor
Berkshire
SL4 3NH
Great Britain

Open Spaces Society
25a Bell Street
Henley-on-Thames
Oxfordshire
RG9 2BA
Great Britain

Ordnance Survey
Romsey Road
Maybush
Southampton
Hampshire
SO16 4GU
Great Britain

Ramblers' Association
1/5 Wandsworth Road
London
SW8 2XX
Great Britain

**Youth Hostels Association
(England and Wales)**
Trevelyan House
8 St Stephens Hill
St Albans
Herts AL1 2DY

**Foundation for Long Distance
Footpaths**
Postbus 846
NL-3800
AV Amersfoort
Holland

Irish Youth Hostels Association
61 Mountjoy Square South
Dublin 7
Ireland

**Federazione Italiana Escur-
sionismo**
via La Spezia 58 r
1-16149 Genova
Italy

Associazione Sentiero Italia
via San Gervasio 12
1-50131
Firenze F1
Italy

Norwegian Mountain Touring Association
Postboks 7 Sentrum
N-0101
Oslo
Norway

Johannesburg Hiking Club
PO Box 786974
Sandton 2146
South Africa

Federacion Espanola de Montana y Escalada
Alberto Aguilera 3-4
E-28015
Madrid
Spain

Federacio d'Entitats Excursionistes de Catalunya
Ramblas 61, Ir
E-08002
Barcelona
Spain

Schweizer Wanderwege
Im Hirshalm 49
CH-4152
Riehen
Switzerland

Swedish Touring Club (STF)
Box 25
S-10120
Stockholm
Sweden

American Hiking Society
1422 Fenwick Lane
Silver Spring
MD 20910
USA

Sierra Club
85 Second Street
Second Floor
San Francisco
CA 94105-3441
USA

American Volkssport Association
Suite 101
Phoenix Square
1001 Pat Booker Road
Universal City
Texas 78148
USA

FURTHER READING

Ashton, Steve. *The Hillwalker's Handbook* (Crowood Press, 1996)

Burton, Anthony. *Best Foot Forward — A guide to planning and enjoying walks in Britain* (Arum Press, 1998)

Duerdon, Frank. *Rambling Complete* (Kaye and Ward, 1978)

Gillman, Peter. *Fitness on Foot* (Sunday Times/World's Work, 1978)

Jebb, Miles. *Walkers* (Constable, 1986)

MacDermid, Heather. *Teach Yourself Walking and Rambling* (Hodder & Stoughton, 1992)

Mitchell, Edwin Valentine, ed. *The Pleasures of Walking* (Spurbooks, 1975)

O'Connor, Bill. *Scrambles in the Lake District* (David & Charles, 1995)

The Rambler's Yearbook and Accommodation Guide (Ramblers' Association, annual)

Smith, Roger. *Simple Map Reading* (The Stationery Office, 1997)

Snowdon, Les and Humphreys, Maggie. *The Walking Diet* (Penguin, 1992)

Stilwell, Tim, ed. *National Trail Companion* (Stilwell Publishing, annual)

Sussman, Aaron and Goode, Ruth. *The Magic of Walking* (Fireside/Simon and Schuster, 1980)

Townsend, Chris. *The Backpacker's Handbook* (Oxford Illustrated Press, 1991)

Townsend, Chris. *A Guide to Hill Walking* (Crowood Press, 1996)

Tully, Clive. *The Trail Walking Handbook* (Blandford, 1994)

Westacott, Hugh. *The Walker's Handbook* (Oxford Illustrated Press, 1989)

Wilson, John G. *Follow the map — the Ordnance Survey guide* (A & C Black and Ordnance Survey, 1985)

INDEX

ACKNOWLEDGEMENTS

Acknowledgements in Source Order

David Bellamy 111; **Brasher** /Hillmaster Antishock Trekking Poles 63 right, /Country Master Classic 35, 41 centre; Campingaz 83 right;

Cicerone Press 36; **Coleman UK Plc** 76, 82 top, 82 bottom; **Columbia Sportswear** 45 right; **Corbis UK Ltd.**/Annie Griffiths 84 right, /Hulton-Deutsch Collection 11, /James Marshall 106, /Marc Muench 72–73, 109, /Phil Scherrmeister 77 left, /Karl Weatherly 64–65; **Craghoppers Ltd.** 38–39, 45 Bottom Left, 50, 96;

Frank Lane Picture Agency/D Dugan 99, /G Marcoaldi/Panda Photo 33 Bottom, 67, /Panda Photo 93, /R Wilmshurst 105, /E Woods 105 Bottom;

Garmin (Europe) Ltd. 71 right; **Gelert** 43 left, 52 left, 61 left, 61 right, 62;

Images Colour Library Limited 22; **Life Systems** 118; **Lowe Alpine** 44, 51 left, 51 Top, 51 Bottom, 56 right, 57 Top, 57 Bottom Left, 57 Bottom Right, 59 Top Left, 59 Top Right, 59 Bottom,

Merrell (Europe) Ltd. 41 Centre Left, 41 Top; **Mountain Range** 80 Top, 80 Bottom, 81;

Neebee/Tareya Boots 40; **Next Destination Ltd.**/Magellan Pioneer GPS 71 left; **North American Race Walking Foundation**/Elaine Ward 23

Octopus Publishing Group Ltd./Mike Busselles 91, /Peter Loughran 102, /Zul Makhida 110, /Tim Woodcock 68; **Ordnance Survey** 66, 69;

Regatta Ltd. 45 Top Left, 49 left, 49 Top Right, 49 Bottom Right, 52 Bottom; **Robert Harding Picture Library**/Shout 114–115; Image Bank/Walter Bibikow 24 Bottom, /Chris Close 107 Bottom; /David De Lossy 27, 28–29, 87, /Per Ericksson 85, /Marc Grimberg 74 Bottom, /Hussey & Hussey 24 Top, /Michael Melford 1, /Terje Rakke 19, 92, /Marc Romanelli 8, /Paul J Sutton 95 Top; **Rohan** 46, 47 left;

Shout 14 Top, 14 Bottom, 15, 17 Top, 18, 20, 30, 31, 34, 41 Bottom, 58 right, 74 Top Left, 74 Top Right, 83, 86, 90 Top, 90 Bottom, 94, 95 Bottom, 97 left, 104, 108, 116, 117, 119 Top, 119 Bottom, 120; **Silva (UK) Ltd.** 53 right, 70, **Snugpak** 78 left, 78 right, 79 Top;

Terra Firma 42 left, 42 right; **Tilley Endurables** 53 left; **Tony Stone Images**/John Beatty Front Cover bottom centre, /Tom Bean 98, /Oliver Benn 107 Top, /Stewart Cohen 26, /Joe Cornish 88–89, /Monica Dalmasso Front Cover background, 43 right, /Richard Elliott 123–124, /Paul Harris 97 right, /John Lawrence 17 Bottom, /David Paterson 2–3, /Lori Adamski-Peek Front Cover bottom left, Front Cover bottom right, 21, 25, 60, /Dave Schiefelbein 4–5, 54–55, /Philip & Karen Smith 12–13, /Tom Stock Front Endpaper, Back Endpaper, 16, 100–101, 113 Top, /Mike Timo 112, /Stuart Westmoreland 103, /Art Wolfe 6–7;

Vango 48, 63 left; **VauDe** 47 right, 75, 77 right, 79 Bottom

Wayfayrer Foods 84 left;

Youth Hostels Association (England & Wales) Ltd. 10, 32, 33 Top, 37, 121, /D Higgs 9, 113 Bottom, /D Jenkins 56 left, /Diane Nightingale Spine, Back Cover